THE WOMEN AROUND JESUS

The Women Around Jesus

Elisabeth Moltmann-Wendel

CROSSROAD · NEW YORK

1997

The Crossroad Publishing Company
370 Lexington Avenue, New York, N.Y. 10017

Translated by John Bowden from the German
Ein eigener Mensch werden. Frauen um Jesus,
published by Gütersloher Verlagshaus Gerd Mohn,
Gütersloh 1980.

First British edition published 1982
by SCM Press Ltd
58 Bloomsbury Street, London WC1B 3QX

Printed in the United States of America

Library of Congress Catalog Card Number: 82-72478

ISBN: 0-8245-0535-2

For my husband

CONTENTS

LIST OF ILLUSTRATIONS

ACKNOWLEDGMENTS

The publisher is grateful to the following for permission to reproduce
illustrations on the pages shown:

Page xii, Ringfoto Wirth, Calw; page 16, City of Nuremberg,
Hauptamt für Hochbauwesen; page 30, The Work of Fra Angelico
in the Museum of San Marco, Officine Grafiche Stianti, Florence;
page 40, Dr Hermann Jantzen, Tübingen; pages 41 and 86, V. Vicari,
Foto-Cine Ottica, Lugano; page 60, Christ Church College, Oxford;
page 62, SCALA Istituto Fotografico Editoriale, Florence; pages
74, 118 and 145, Georg Goerlipp, Donaueschingen; page 106,
Jugenddienst-Verlag, Wuppertal; page 130, Staatliche Graphische
Sammlung-Photothek, Munich.

It is time that the church acquitted women of Eve's 'sin', since it has even forgiven the Jews for their 'crime'.

Elizabeth Gould-Davis

Among the historical limitations of the biblical writings is the fact that they were composed by men. What, for example, might a history of Israel look like if portrayed and written from the perspective of wives and mothers, who were allowed neither to bear weapons nor to join in worship?

Kurt Marti

Seventy-seven biblical women turn to Christ

The Bridal Procession of the Shulamite.
Protestant Church of the Holy Trinity in Bad Teinach, 1673.

INTRODUCTION

Women discover themselves in the Bible

Some years ago, unusual religious services were held in Solentiname in Nicaragua under the direction of the priest-poet Ernesto Cardenal. Families of farmers and fishermen met together, read a text from the Bible and then talked spontaneously about it, all with a heightened awareness of the need for social change, of the injustices inflicted on them by the social system, and of Christ, the liberator of the oppressed.

One Sunday, part of the Easter story was read aloud, about how the women came to the tomb to anoint the body of Jesus. The peasant women got excited and began to identify themselves with these women: 'It was the women who went to the tomb first, and not the men; women are braver than men.' 'Women have more heart. And love can make you very strong. When you love, you have no fear and can cope with anyone. Jesus, who died for love, gave them this courage, the courage of love. When you love, you're bold. You're not even afraid of death.'

What happened next seems to me to be typical of Christian communities right down the ages: the men protested that the women were laying claim to a special role: 'I don't see that the women were all that brave . . . what was so tremendous about going there and weeping for a while? . . .'

The spontaneous reaction of the women was repressed, and Cardenal the theologian provided the historical reason for this: in fact it was not so dangerous for women to be at the tomb as

1

it was for men. The women yielded a bit, and a 'partnership' was arrived at. ('Of course the women played a very important role, as did the men. However, that does not mean that they were braver or loved Jesus more.')

There are three important aspects to this brief episode. First, the spontaneous way in which women can rediscover themselves in the Bible. Secondly, the emotional and zealous concern of men that women should not arrive at too much self-awareness. Thirdly, that historical reasons had to be produced to stabilize the male role.

In this unconventional service, the women read the Bible with their own eyes and rediscovered themselves there. They rediscovered the special role which Jesus accorded to women, and came to understand something of the old New Testament tradition about women. How can we, too, rediscover this spontaneity in our turn?

Stories about women in the New Testament

First of all, let us consider the New Testament tradition about women. This is familiar to some women who have spent a number of years studying the Bible. However, many women have found the Bible to be more a force in maintaining the existing order than a book of liberation: it says that 'woman' is to be silent in church, is 'blessed through bearing children', 'led man astray' and 'was the first to sin'. Given these well-known statements, how can we be free and aware of ourselves, while regarding the Bible as being on the side of women? It is because of this that women alienated from the Bible and the church follow August Bebel and Simone de Beauvoir in looking on the Bible as the chief instrument in the suppression of women.

However, over the past few years, above all in the USA, so much noteworthy research has been carried out by women that we may take it as certain that Jesus had a unique relationship

2

with women and that as a result of this, in many early communities there was an unusual social equality of men and women. Granted, this episode did not last long, and presumably the development did not take place everywhere. Still, a number of investigations, the reading of sources in a new light, and above all the heightened awareness among women of their history has now unfolded for us a picture of an early Christian community consisting of women with the same status as men. Apostles like Junia, women like Phoebe exercising the functions of a bishop, leading women Christians like Mary Magdalene, change our view of the role of women in Christianity, established and dictated, as it has been, by the fact of their sex. What happened here was not just a gesture of goodwill towards women, not just a domestic recognition, but a change in sexual roles and in social functions.

Psychoanalytical research has demonstrated that Jesus was the only man not dominated by the *animus*; Hanna Wolff calls him 'the integrated man', i.e. a man who integrated and brought to maturity the masculine and feminine attitudes which are to be found in any human being. As a result of this he was capable of entering into a more absolute partnership with women. This does not mean that he was any the less the Son of God. It simply enables us to have a better understanding of the psychological and social side of the story of Jesus and to incorporate it into our own existence. Something new happened here, in contrast to all other founders of religions, however well-disposed towards women they may have been: it was a form of liberating acceptance which had social consequences. It broke down the 'androcentrism' of the ancient world, to use Hanna Wolff's term, i.e. the masculine orientation, the adoption of masculine models and standards. The coming of Jesus released new values. Since his life and ministry we have been freed from old standards; new patterns of behaviour have been opened up to us. This affects many areas of human life. However, the question of women is a decisive sphere in which

3

new things could come about and will continue to come about.

History tends to be understood as 'his story', the story of males, and Christian history also tends to be regarded from this perspective, though it once began as the history of men *and* women. Men made history. Paul and Peter shaped the churches, and the Bible hands down to us what they thought about God and about liberation through Jesus. In this history of masculine activity, women get a very raw deal. For the most part they appear in the weaker social roles; they serve as widows, appear as sisters and wives. Males make remarks about them, about their refusal to wear veils, say that they ought to obey the rules rather than join in making them, that they should not be arrogant and presumptuous.

But where do women have a say? What would history, or church history, look like if it were written from their point of view? Where is 'her story' in the Bible? A history written by women and regarded from a feminine perspective?

In recent years, continual attempts have been made to look at stories and histories from a different perspective, from that of people who would otherwise be dumb: the oppressed or the illiterate. The history of colonialism as told by a slave, e.g. in the American television serial *Roots*, looks very different from the viewpoint of the masters as represented, say, in *Gone with the Wind*. The history of the working class to be found in August Kuhn's book *Zeit zum Aufstehen* (Time to Rebel, 1977) shows us a different way of looking at industrialization and its consequences from that of the middle classes. The history of women at different periods, e.g. the history of the pioneer women in the United States, their hopes, their suffering, their fates, sheds new light on the world of cowboys and Westerns. This greatly varied 'underside', the historical underworld, exercises a fascination today: minorities have their say; forgotten sources are opened up; stories acquire a new value; symbols, images and other 'wordless' traditions again find a means of expression. The underside of history does not have the powerful instruments of paper and writing at its disposal.

In view of all that we know about the uniqueness of the story of Jesus, 'her story' in the New Testament has a special significance. However, it is subject to the same laws as the other unwritten histories of minorities. We are now groping in an attempt to discover what can still be known about women of the past; we are attempting to acquire a new understanding of what has been written about women; presuming that women were more active than has hitherto been supposed, even in writing. Are there perhaps parts of the Gospels, or even parts of the New Testament, which were written by women? At least the most important traditions, i.e. those of the death, burial and resurrection of Jesus, go back to women, because they were the only followers of Jesus who were there at the time. The great scholar Adolf von Harnack conjectured that a woman, Priscilla, wrote the Epistle to the Hebrews. Later books, which were not included in the Bible, at least have women as their subjects (Thecla, Mary Magdalene), and have preserved voices and sayings of which we would otherwise be ignorant.

It is now generally agreed that much material about or written by women was lost or destroyed in the church's struggle with Gnosticism. Women often enjoyed more respect in Gnostic circles than in the mainstream church which was gradually coming into being. The mainstream church, adapted to the patriarchal social structures of society, did not offer women the same opportunities as Gnostic groups. So in the ideological controversies, women too came to grief. Accordingly, the tradition about women in the Jesus movement emerges from our Bible as no more than the tip of an iceberg. However, this tip is clearly visible, more clearly than in other corresponding documents of world literature. There is some evidence that women, and not the disciples, were the real followers of Jesus. At all events, women played a unique role in his last days, and according to most of the evidence – Paul, in I Cor. 15.5, is an exception – they were probably also the first witnesses of his resurrection. The Bible has within its pages a unique history of the greatness, the sovereignty, the wisdom and the courage of women. It is perhaps the most interesting book in connection with the emancipation of women.

The women of Solentiname knew this.

Personal and social changes

But how do we gain access to the Bible? How do we regain our lost spontaneity?

No tradition can have an effect unless it is understood in a particular situation. In other words, had not the women in Nicaragua felt that they were in a revolutionary situation, they would not have found it possible to rediscover in the Bible their state of persecution, their guerrilla fighting, the suffering and persecution of their families and their personal powers of endurance. They read the Bible in a situation which was changed for them, both personally and socially. Transferred to our situation, this means that 'her story' will not arouse a spark of interest without the experience that there is discrimination against women, that they are relegated to a secondary position in society and in the church. Relegation, discrimination means that they cannot make their own contribution, that they are continually confined to particular 'feminine' roles, though it has long been demonstrated that women can be 'masculine', just as men can be 'feminine'. Our bourgeois, patriarchal church and society is now being questioned from all sides. A post-industrial society is coming into being. In such transitional situations, people read the Bible with new eyes, gain a new understanding and find it liberating because they feel personally affected. Luther found in the Bible the justification of the godless, and as a result, for him the clerical social order and the demands of the conscience of the individual underwent a change. Josephine Butler, the English pioneer in the struggle for the vote for women, who carried on a successful fight against state-sponsored prostitution, read it as the great book of liberation which proclaimed the same justice for men and women. For her the word 'redemption' was too weak to express what Jesus had brought to women.

Today, people in many parts of the world have begun to read the Bible as a book of minorities. It has been rediscovered in Western culture as the book of 'tenderness', to use Heinrich Böll's phrase, i.e. of a more sensitive mutual relationship among human beings. In theology, attempts are being made to arrive at a new understanding of the biblical text by materialistic, psycho-analytical or feminist interpretations. None of them is to be taken as absolute, but each of them enriches our approach. The Bible is no longer the book that stabilizes government and confirms the existing order. It has fallen into the hands of the powerless, and the question is what it has to say to them and what 'power' it gives them: a new, old 'mastery', or the power of those who remained by the cross.

Difficulties with a patriarchal tradition

When all this has been said, this 'revolutionary' tradition about women cannot be seen all that easily, and I would like to follow Maria de Groot (*Frauen auf neuen Wegen*, ed. G. Scharffenorth, Gelnhausen 1978, p. 221), in saying that even progressive feminist groups often do not see what underlies the Bible, regarded in a traditional way. It is necessary to warn against euphoria. We are not just dealing with male emotions. In our tradition, particularly in matters concerning women, we have to cart off various layers of rubble before we arrive at the treasure chamber.

Let me draw attention to some of these difficulties.

1. The Bible was written, or at least given its final form, in a predominantly patriarchal culture. It contains a number of sexist remarks, i.e. remarks which suppress women, e.g. in the Old Testament, which sees the wife as her husband's personal

property. In the late writings even of the New Testament she is once again burdened with 'Eve's sin'. In a patriarchal society, preference is given to this patriarchal superstructure, and it is used for the political suppression of women.

2. A long accepted view of the Bible, which is mostly hostile to women, has given form to a history of the tradition which has made a deep mark on human consciousness. Women are associated with sexuality and sin (Mary Magdalene), cooking and housekeeping (Martha), and motherhood (Mary). Women in the Bible are not allowed any beauty, independence or originality of their own, and are made to fulfil the function of providing whatever image of womanhood Christianity may desire. Where this does not work – for example, with the women of the Old Testament who engaged in politics and made history, Deborah, Judith and Miriam – the women concerned went off to find a place in literature and were lost to the church's tradition.

3. Even modern interpretation and preaching often begins with a presupposition of what women should be: receptive like Mary, active like Martha, or restrained like Mary of Bethany.

4. The Bible study familiar in the women's movement since the 1920s, and still practised today, began from accepted ways of thinking. Thus in 1935, Vikarin Jonas wrote: 'Our women . . . must become acquainted with the biblical ordinances: What does scripture say about the creation of the world, the Fall, about man and woman and their relationship to each other . . .' '. . . the position of woman must come to the fore . . .' (Fritz Mybes, *Geschichte der Evangelischen Frauenhilfe in Quellen*, Gladbach 1975). At the same time this meant a new rational adoption of the Bible, its words and its concepts.

In 1935, a woman reported: 'We now had to learn to read history word for word, to ask about everything that we could not understand . . . how often in the past we had simply let our ideas run riot.' The motto is 'to stand under the Bible, not over it'. Questions about the 'scope' of the text, its christological significance, made access to the Bible too one-sided, too logical, too rational. There was only *one* way of approaching it: theo-*logical* and christo*logical*. In this first phase of their activity in the church, women had to turn their backs on imaginative, simply human approaches to the Bible, stamped with feeling and experience.

There is a long tradition of seeing the Bible as a book of comfort, a book which brings security to governments and confirms and interprets law and order. This still has an effect. So for centuries the Bible has been used to keep women under control. Just as in the most recent past Romans 13 was used to legitimate any government, no matter how shameful it may have been, so too it served to keep women at home. Those who experience God as a power for order can always misuse the Bible to secure their ends.

Imagination

Reading the Bible as a book of liberation may find approval, but women will hardly succeed in this all by themselves. We cannot quickly obviate the difficulties, outlined above, in a patriarchal situation which extends from social interests in the subordination of women, through unconscious presuppositions, to the inculcated need for a rational approach to the Bible.

If we are to regain the access we have lost, the spontaneity of which we have been deprived, we must learn once again to think, feel, live and act in terms of a total sense of living. To do this, we shall have to rediscover a forgotten art to use our imagination in our theology. Theological imagination is neces-sary in a church and a theology which has lost touch with women, if new life is to be given to the gospel of liberation. With this kind of imagination, theology which has become abstract and has lost touch with women can again become what it once was, and affect the whole person. Such imagination is the power of the Holy Spirit to bring to new life whatever has become fossilized. However, people have never really trusted women in the church with this power. That is all the more reason why we should develop our spirituality, our trust in the spirit, and our trust in ourselves.

Here are some possibilities for such a theological imagination.

1. To use art and culture to rediscover obscured traditions which are matriarchal, or favourable to women: Mary who rides on the lion; Mary Magdalene, the beautiful friend of Jesus; Martha, who defeats the dragon (see below).

2. To attempt to re-integrate into the reality of church and society those women of the Old Testament who have found their place in literature rather than the church's tradition.

3. To take a new look at the biblical stories about women, considering their human features, their biographies, their personalities, without concern for christological features or any references to Jesus. As Letty Russell says: 'Watch it like a movie!'

4. To work out by means of these stories our own developing understanding of Christian society; to ask how they once struck us, and how they strike us now.

5. To have the courage to be subjective and openly to reject those passages in the Bible which are hostile to women or ill-disposed towards them. To identify masculine writers like Paul, Luke and John, and to judge how they experienced women's liberation and how they realized it in their communities.

6. To have the freedom to change patriarchal metaphors into feminist ones: to replace son by daughter, father by mother; and to discover new metaphors.

7. To interpret the Bible as a whole, i.e. in terms of a feminine sense of living, that is, not with feelings of alienation, sin and guilt, but with feelings of being accepted and being healed. Maria de Groot attempts this mystical interpretation: God and I on one side, death and sin on the other.

8. To retell history with new narrative forms, new ways of

bringing it home to an audience, dramatic representations, and in so doing to give it a life of its own which stands alongside our own lives. Where God is experienced as a liberating force, the Bible discloses countless new possibilities.

About this book

This book attempts to remove the burden of the patriarchal past from a small section of the New Testament. I was prompted to write it by feminist groups who – aroused by the contemporary feminist movement – wanted to discover something new about the women in the New Testament. Feminist theologians have recently already given a good deal of thought to the 'other Mary' (e.g. C. Halkes, *Una Sancta*, 1977 (4), 32nd Year), which does not fit into the pattern of accepted Mariology. However, this did not touch the hearts of my Protestant sisters. They were used to identifying with others of the women around Jesus: Martha, Mary of Bethany, Mary Magdalene. These had evidently been the instruments in a long history of Protestant education: into proficiency, modesty, humility and receptiveness. This was disturbing.

So this book begins with Martha, whom I learned to see with new eyes, first through the Bible, then in art and in church history. The illustrations should show us the 'other' woman who is hidden from us by the patriarchal view of history and the blinkers worn by the church, and should guide us back to the other possibilities offered by the Christian traditions. To look back, however, is at the same time to look forward: in today's social conditions women in the church are not on their own. They have a wide-ranging tradition to which they can refer. While even the commentaries, most of which have been written by men, are historically conditioned, they are not completely hopeless: all through them we keep finding a recognition which was in conflict with the traditional role of women.

The biblical references are largely taken from the *Good News*

Bible. Where this has been inadequate, I have made my own translations.

Finally, I would like to thank all those who have helped with advice about the writing of this book, with looking for texts and pictures, and above all my family, whose serendipity has enriched it considerably.

Martha as we know her . . .

Martha Serving at Table.
The Magdalene Altar at Tiefenbronn, by Lucas Moser, 1431.

1

MARTHA

As Jesus and his disciples went on their way, he came to a village where a woman named Martha welcomed him in her home. She had a sister named Mary, who sat down at the feet of the Lord and listened to his teaching. Martha was upset over all the work she had to do, so she came and said, 'Lord, don't you care that my sister has left me to do all the work by myself? Tell her to come and help me.' The Lord answered her, 'Martha, Martha! You are worried and troubled over so many things, but just one is needed. Mary has chosen the right thing, and it will not be taken away from her' (Luke 10.38–42).

Now there was a sick man, Lazarus of Bethany, from the village of Mary and her sister Martha . . . The sisters told Jesus, 'Your friend is sick.' When Jesus heard that, he said, 'This sickness will not lead to death, but to the glory of God. God will use it to manifest the glory of his Son.'

Jesus loved Mary and her sister, and Lazarus. But when he heard the news that Lazarus was sick, he stayed where he was for two more days. Then he said to his disciples, 'We shall return to Judaea.' He added: 'Our friend Lazarus has fallen asleep. But I shall go and wake him.' . . . When Jesus arrived in Bethlehem, Lazarus had already been in the tomb for four days. The village was no more than two miles from Jerusalem, and many Jews had visited Martha and Mary to comfort them. When Martha heard that Jesus was approaching the village, she

... and in unfamiliar guise

Martha Defeating the Dragon.
Church of St Laurence, Nuremberg. Mary Altar, 1517.

went to meet him. Mary stayed at home. Martha said to Jesus, 'Lord, if you had been with us, my brother need not have died. But I know that God will not refuse you anything, even now.' Jesus said to her, 'Your brother will rise again.' 'I know that he will rise again at the last day,' she replied; 'at the general resurrection he too will return to life.' Jesus said to her: 'I am the resurrection and the life. He who believes in me will live, even though he dies. And he who lives and believes in me will never die. Do you believe that?' She said to him, 'Yes Lord, I believe that you are Christ, the Son of God, who has come into the world.' When she had said this she went away, took her sister Mary to one side, and said, 'The Teacher is here and is calling for you.' When Mary heard that, she quickly arose and ran out to him . . . When Mary came to Jesus and saw him, she threw herself at his feet and said, 'Lord, if you had been with us, my brother need not have died.' Jesus saw her weeping . . . he became angry and was very concerned. 'Where is he lying?', he asked her. He went to the tomb. It was a cave, and the entrance had been sealed with a stone. 'Take the stone away,' he commanded. Martha, the sister of the dead man, objected: 'Lord, he will be stinking. He has already been in the tomb for four days.' Jesus said, 'But I told you, you would see the glory of God if you would only believe.' They took the stone away. Jesus looked up to heaven and said, 'I thank you, Father, for fulfilling my prayer. I am saying this aloud because of the people here, so that they may believe that you have sent me.' After these words, he cried aloud, 'Lazarus, come forth.' And the dead man came forth (John 11.1–44, abbreviated).

The most zealous Christians, the priests, find . . . that we should join Martha in serving, rather than offering to the Lord the vessel of our life with all the fragrance that it contains (Thérèse of Lisieux).

Martha, your work must be punished and counted as nought

17

. . . I will have no work but the work of Mary; that is the faith that you have in the Word (Martin Luther).

Martha first notices that Jesus is coming, runs to meet him, talks a great deal, and in so doing makes a full confession of faith, and then points out that the dead man is already rotting, so that Jesus has to rebuke her (Johannes Leipoldt).

The closest parallel to that confession (of Peter's) . . . appears on the lips of a woman, Martha . . . Thus, if other Christian communities thought of Peter as the one who made a supreme confession of Jesus as the Son of God and the one to whom the risen Jesus first appeared, the Johannine communities associated such reminiscences with heroines like Martha (Raymond Brown).

Martha's reply shows the true attitude of faith, in that she avoids saying anything about life, completely disregards herself, and only speaks of 'You', that is, of the one who has encountered her as God's Revealer and whom she recognizes as such in faith. She cannot see the life that gives promise, but she can recognize that in Jesus God's eschatological intervention in the world is taking place (Rudolf Bultmann).

Useful, but worth-less

When I think of 'Martha', a picture from a children's Bible comes to mind. In it, Mary is sitting at Jesus' feet and listening to him, while in the background Martha is leaning against the kitchen door with an evil, mistrustful look on her face.

As a child, I was always sorry for anyone called Martha. The name has connotations of being especially alert, active, earthy, plump, jolly and competent. 'I'd rather have been called Ruth,' my friend Martha would say to me.

There was something noble about 'Mary', 'Martha' was

rather common. Mary had an aura of holiness, whereas Martha breathed cooking and the smell of the kitchen.

Even now you can sometimes hear older people say, 'She's the Martha type', by which they mean that she is particularly practical, competent, down-to-earth. Or, 'She's the Mary type', which means that she is quiet, restrained, a good listener, always receptive to others.

If we are honest, Martha is presented to us as being useful and necessary. But when it comes to a model, a comfort or an ideal, it's Mary all the time.

Let us remind ourselves of the story which gives rise to these different feelings for the two sisters.

Jesus comes to Bethany and visits Mary and Martha. Martha, who does the housekeeping, rushes off to the kitchen to prepare a meal for the guest. Mary sits at Jesus' feet and listens to him. When Martha notices that Mary is not helping, she complains to Jesus, and Jesus takes Mary's side: one thing only is needed; Mary has chosen the good portion . . . This seems to have devalued Martha's activity and presented Mary's attitude as the model.

This story gives rise to our different feelings about the two sisters from Bethany, and these different feelings can be found time and again in the Christian tradition. Because she sat at Jesus' feet and listened to him, Mary became the type of the contemplative, i.e. the reflective Christian. Reflection was of greater value than any Christian activism. In church we still sing, 'O Lord, one thing alone we need; teach me, I pray, your voice to heed.'

Here are some lines about Mary:

> One thing alone thought Mary meet,
> enrapt she sat at Jesus' feet,
> her heart aflame to hear the word
> imparted by her dearest Lord.
> No eye but for her Saviour's face,
> so she was given his fullest grace.

19

THE WOMEN AROUND JESUS

Mary combines 'simplicity and humility', as the hymn goes on to say, and in so doing attains supreme wisdom. She leaves behind all that is earthly and 'soars above nature'. She loves Jesus and gives herself totally to him. Even away from such mystical love for Jesus, in Reformed Christianity, Mary's standing is high. From Luther down to the present-day commentators Mary has exemplified someone who is good and righteous before God because she listened to the word.

Not so Martha. There are no hymns about Martha. Because she went into the kitchen to prepare a meal for Jesus, her guest, she has been relegated to cooking and housekeeping. She has been made the patron saint of housewives and cooks, and been given a saint's day (29 July). Even now there are Martha Organizations, for domestics in manses and guest-houses. A women's movement in England which is opposed to the emancipation of women is called the Martha Movement. Martha was painted as a housekeeper with a key-ring, and as a cook in a great Dutch Renaissance kitchen. Thus she still had a useful function in the mediaeval Catholic doctrine of estates, in which each estate was divinely willed and was part of an order of which God approved.

However, she hardly reached the higher ranks of spirituality. Because she was practical, she was also associated with the care of the sick, and in this way she became the patron saint of those who nursed the sick. Churches were rarely named after her. Above Lugano there is a half-ruined Martha church, built by an order of lay brothers who wanted to dedicate themselves to the care of those suffering from the plague. In the interior, Martha is portrayed as a nurse clothed in white, dedicating lay brothers. But this is an unknown church and an almost unknown lay order on the periphery of the great spiritual communities. In Nuremberg there is a small mediaeval Martha church which belonged to a pilgrims' hospital.

Here too, Martha is regarded as a patron saint concerned with activism. In art, Martha is usually portrayed as a maternal,

20

domestic saint: she serves at table, prays, and motherly tranquillity radiates from her. As a saint, Martha fulfils all the desires people have for a wife and mother. If Mary is the embodiment of reflective, contemplative Christianity, Martha is the embodiment of active Christianity.

Things only worsened when Protestant theologians got hold of Martha. For the Reformers, and even for many commentators today, Martha is the embodiment of righteousness by works. She wants to do something for Jesus – and that is wrong. For God makes us righteous by grace, and takes no account of our good works. Thus the image of Martha became very complicated: useful in practical matters, but less useful than the thoughtful Mary, and thus 'worth-less'. Consequently many women in the church, who even now tend to identify with Martha, feel that they are less valuable, even worthless, and develop inferiority complexes.

However, when in the last century the values of active Christianity and Christian service were rediscovered, Martha was rediscovered too. An active image of women was needed for social workers and deaconesses involved in Christian service. Mary, who only listened, was no longer enough. A disciple of Zinzendorf, for whom 'listening to the Word' was not enough, added a new verse to Zinzendorf's hymn 'Lord, Thy Word a noble gift'.

> Grant me, Lord, the zeal to labour,
> night and day, in cold and heat,
> and the grace thy word to savour,
> rapt, like Mary, at thy feet.

So arose the double role of Mary and Martha. The pioneer of women's emancipation, Louise Otto-Peters, also wanted to be both: a disciple like Mary *and* Martha. A pastor produced the verse,

> Martha and Mary in one life
> Make up the perfect vicar's wife

And Wichern wrote that 'Martha must be a Mary and the true Mary must also be a Martha; both are sisters'. This was making a virtue out of necessity. In fact the Martha Houses of the deaconess organizations were the domestic houses, and Martha no more succeeded in receiving her due in the church than did the deaconesses. Martha and her homeliness are still on the periphery of our Christianity as it celebrates, thinks and meditates, just as the Martha Houses are on the periphery of the great deaconess organizations.

The forgotten Martha

Now this tradition does a great injustice to Martha, and it is time that we put it right. If we look at the Bible and the passages where Martha occurs, there are in fact two quite different Martha stories. They are told in two different Gospels and by different men: one by Luke; the other, about ten years later, by John. Luke reports the better-known story of Martha who serves and Mary who listens, and to whom Jesus pays a visit; John tells the story of the raising of Lazarus, the brother of Mary and Martha. Both agree in recording that the two sisters were very different. One, Mary, was quiet, restrained, even a bit withdrawn. The other, Martha, was active, used to giving orders, quick, eloquent, and with a tendency to be bossy towards her shy sister. The communities in which both Luke and John lived still remembered two women who were close to Jesus, different in their gifts, with quite different characters and different functions. Furthermore, one was particularly active in the early community, perhaps too active and self-possessed, as we shall soon see. Her particular responsibility must have been diaconal functions: serving at table at the eucharist, administrative work, looking after the poor.

Both Luke and John were, as authors of the early church, well-disposed to women. As Greek Christians they were familiar with the involvement of women in the society of the time

22

and were in sympathy with it. Others, like Matthew and Mark, Jewish Christians who lived in communities in which women played more traditional roles, seem – at first glance – to be less interested in individual women. However, both Luke and John see women and the work of women from a particular perspective. Luke had a weakness for rich, prominent women, and Mary and Martha accorded well with this. Martha is called lady of the house. From all that we can infer from the texts, she was a well-to-do landowner, who looked after the family estate. Luke also tells us of other prominent women, otherwise unknown to us, who were disciples of Jesus and financed either him or the community. For example, there is Lydia, who deals in purple dyes; and Joanna, the minister's wife, who had left her husband, King Herod's Minister of Finance, and despite her high status remained with Jesus, the enemy of the state, until his death and then Easter. The early church is unthinkable for Luke without the active, influential and well-to-do women around Jesus.

Luke was also sufficiently sympathetic to write a special sermon for women and also took account of women's needs: because the traditional parables of Jesus were too predominantly taken from the sphere of masculine work, he corrected the balance by introducing parables about women's activities (baking bread, spring cleaning, looking for a lost coin, and so on).

John took the part of women even more strongly. Nowadays, his Gospel is a treasure trove for a tradition about women in the early church which was later forgotten: he tells the story of the woman of Samaria, who became the first apostle to the Gentiles. He has Jesus, on the cross, pass on his heritage to a man and a woman, John and Mary his mother, both of whom, of equal status, are the symbolic embodiment of the new community. And he tells a different version of the story of Mary and Martha, which has become so much a part of us.

Let us remind ourselves of John's story: Lazarus is sick, and

Mary and Martha let Jesus know of his friend's illness – probably in the hope that Jesus will come and make him better. When Jesus eventually sets off, five days later, Lazarus has already been dead for four days. In the packed house of mourning, Martha hears of his coming, takes the initiative, and leaves the house to meet Jesus by herself. She rushes up to Jesus with a remark which contains all the grief, all the anger and all the disappointment of the last few days: 'Lord, if you had been here, my brother need not have died.' Mary says the same thing later, as she casts herself at Jesus' feet – and then immediately bursts into tears. For Martha, however, this remark is a springboard, the introduction to a passionate conversation about faith. Martha is not 'a woman' who 'keeps silence' in the community. She does not leave theology to the theologians. She carries on a vigorous debate. She does not cry, she does not cast herself at Jesus' feet, she does not give in. She struggles with God as Job did. She charges Jesus with failure. She does not give up, just as Jacob did not give up at the Jabbok, when he was wrestling with God. In her mind, she knows well enough that theologically resurrection takes place only at the Last Day, yet she hopes that Jesus can help now.

Forward, stubborn, passionate – she knows it all better. Many people would call this un-feminine. At least she does not incorporate any traditional feminine Christian virtues: obedience, tranquillity, subservience. These are characteristic, rather, of Mary. She stays in the house, joins the relatives in mourning her brother, and has to be summoned by her sister. In tears, she chokes out her timid protest to Jesus: 'If you had been with us, my brother need not have died.'

One commentator, who has been particularly concerned with women in the New Testament (Leipoldt), remarks at this point: 'Mary feels it much more deeply than Martha.' But is not this a presupposition, a prejudiced view of what a woman and her faith should be: obedient, recognizing the limitations, asking nothing more, doubting nothing, falling into line? John, though,

24

wanted to portray quite a different woman: the rebel, who does not toe the line, who will not be satisfied with what a man says to her. Bultmann is right here: it is Martha who has the stronger faith.

Martha – a leading Christian

Jesus responds to Martha's stubborn, passionate faith that he is no ordinary person with the revelation of himself, 'I am the resurrection and the life . . .', and Martha responds with a confession of Christ which stands out as a special climax in the New Testament: 'You are Christ, the Son of God, who has come into the world.' At most this can be compared with Peter's confession of Christ in Matthew 16.16.

Thus John placed the confession of Christ on the lips of a woman, a woman who was known for her openness, her strength and her practical nature. This is a confession of Christ which takes similar form only once more in the other Gospels, where it is uttered by Peter. For the early church, to confess Christ in this way was the mark of an apostle. The church was built up on Peter's confession, and to this day the Popes understand themselves as Peter's successors.

However, we must conclude from this story and this confession that Martha is also a leading personality, like the apostles in the early church. She was a tenacious, wise, combative, competent, emancipated woman with many practical responsibilities in the community. She had a strong sense of reality ('the body is already rotting'!) and was good at organization: 'The teacher is here and is calling for you,' she says to Mary, although he hasn't said a word. Still, we should not imagine her on a bishop's throne or with apostolic status, but as a normal housewife or mistress of the house.

John wanted to use Martha to portray the strength of faith; for him, Mary was the weaker of the two, the average woman. He saw strength in the competent extravert. As far as he was concerned, the church needed women who were aware of themselves. At a time when women were already markedly repressed in the churches, he erected a further memorial to the wise and active woman who was aware of herself. At a time when the male apostolate was taking over in the early period what had been charismatic offices, he once again brought to mind the early story of Jesus, when women had been granted freedom, equality and sisterhood.

In doing this, John throws overboard our traditional Christian image of Martha: he restores to life the aggressive, disturbing, sage, active Martha who went against all the conventions: mistress of the house, housewife, apostle, the woman who stands beside Peter in her own right.

Presumably, as far as we know, this Martha never preached, but her spiritual power of judgment was recognized in the community. Presumably she knew more about housekeeping than about the Old Testament, yet she had the same status and the same importance as her male colleagues.

Today we are discovering that in view of the realities of their experience women can speak of God, of faith, of the fellowship of Christian life in a different way from the theology and the theologians of many centuries. Women have their own sphere of life and their own experience, in which they come to know God and trace his freedom. God is not just strong, almighty and successful; he is also weak and impotent in the way that women are. Perhaps they are often closer to the reality of the new life, the reality of the resurrection, than men. At any rate, the New Testament says clearly that women are at an advantage here: women were the first witnesses to the resurrection; and Martha was the first to experience that Jesus himself is the resurrection.

Why have we forgotten this Martha? Perhaps she caused anxiety to many contemporaries. Perhaps Luke himself is an instance of this; perhaps the competence of Martha forced him to raise a warning finger when he told the other story of Mary and Martha: too much competence, too much emancipation is a dangerous thing. Look at Mary! Model yourself on Mary! Modesty and restraint in the community are better suited to women.

Our Christian tradition has followed Luke. We have kept on telling Luke's version and forgotten that of John. And we have rediscovered ourselves in Martha, the one who is useful, the one who serves, but is clearly of secondary importance.

Of course women will always differ from one another; some will be stronger and some will be weaker, some will be more introvert and some more extravert. The only problem will be if all of them follow the same model.

Luke represents a two-thousand-year-old masculine tradition in our church which is 'well disposed' towards women; it says that the church needs women, and at the same time becomes afraid when women prove to be too independent, too strong, too concerned for equal rights. For too long we have been Marthas, useful and necessary, but without self-awareness, so that we can see all this clearly today. Consequently we should put Luke's Martha in second place and give John's Martha true recognition: we should see her as the woman who is self-aware, active, matter-of-fact; who does not give in, who does not recognize any limitations, who transcends herself and her traditional feminine role and in so doing experiences resurrection.

We have forgotten this Martha. But she enjoyed a long life in the tradition of the early church and in pictorial art. According to an ancient legend, Martha, who persevered until Jesus disclosed himself to her as the resurrection and the life and restored her brother to life, overcame a dragon – a dragon who was the embodiment of evil, the demonic and the old order. In the Middle Ages she was often painted as the proud housewife, with a fettered dragon stretched out at her feet.

Normally it is a man, George, who is known as the one who got the better of the dragon. However, a woman also proved victor over the monster: the Johannine Martha, who was the first to hear that Jesus is the resurrection and the life. This Martha was able to restore to women their lost sense of themselves in the church. So now we could replace the old picture of Martha – looking out of the kitchen with an air of mistrust – with another one: Martha, with the emblems of a housewife, who conquers the old order in the guise of a dragon.

Mediaeval pictures of Martha

(i) Martha the wise virgin

Round about 1300, Meister Eckhart, mystic and Dominican monk, preached on Luke's story of Mary and Martha; he praised the mature Martha and criticized Mary because she was not ready. In so doing he stood traditional interpretation on its head. Up to that point, in traditional commentaries Martha was the negative, the weaker, image compared with the perfect symbol of Mary. She was the image of the Jewish church in comparison with the church of Christ; the image of the imperfect earthly church in comparison with the heavenly church; the image of the active life in contrast to the contemplative life. In comparison with the lofty spiritual claims of the church, she bore the burdens of transitoriness and earthiness. In herself, Martha was nothing. Martha had to be overcome. Now Meister Eckhart visibly distorted this history, and the sophistries which he used to do so are a sign of the strength of the tradition which he had to attack. However, with this foray he displaced Mary and set Martha on the throne. For him she was the true, mature, fulfilled person. She embodied the supreme human ideal and became the shining vision of perfect humanity. Martha is 'mature'. Martha is alive. Martha is active and creative. She does not just work, because 'Working is something external; creativity is when a person with all due perception is involved from within; such people are in the midst of things and yet do not live in things.'

MARTHA

Meister Eckhart suspected that Mary sat by Jesus more out of pleasure than out of a desire to advance in spirituality! First she has to learn to live. Her contentment in enjoying herself, listening, taking things in, falls short of life. It is only the first step towards it. She has chosen 'the good portion', but this is only a promise that one day she will be as mature and as perfect as Martha.

Martha – mature, active and sovereign – arouses utter astonishment in Meister Eckhart: 'What a wondrous involvement both outwardly and inwardly: understanding and being understood; seeing and being seen; holding and being held; that is the last stage where the Spirit perseveres in rest, united to beloved eternity.'

The old ideal of the introvert, receptive woman fades into the background, and Martha emerges from the shadows. With her Meister Eckhart paints a new picture of woman: the picture of the woman who acts responsibly, who is concerned for the world and for her duties. At this time the brilliant image of Mary Magdalene, which embraced many traditional feminine types, still continued to attract the majority of artists. But when faced with the competition offered by Martha, it had to yield. For the first time Martha, who had become discredited since the days of the early church, again began to gain respect. It is impossible to say how widely Meister Eckhart's vivid sermon about Martha was known. At all events, it was in keeping with the spirit of the age, and became the model for a late mediaeval tradition which attached an increased value to women. Although it is well known as the period of the persecution of witches and the time of the great church fathers who condemned women to silence, there was more to the Middle Ages than we suspect.

From the twelfth century onwards, all over Europe, we encounter religious feminist movements which continued down to the end of the Middle Ages. They were part of the revolutionary religious and social movements, and accorded

Martha watches with Christ

The Prayer of Jesus in the Garden of Gethsemane.
Fra Angelico, Monastery of San Marco, Florence.

Martha cradles Lazarus on her lap

Martha, Lazarus and Maximinus after landing at Marseilles. The Magdalene Altar at Tiefenbronn, by Lucas Moser, 1431.

with the trends of the time, representing a move away from the previous hierarchical orders of the church and the unworldly ideals of the cloister towards a new religious life in the world. This religious life was intended to be true discipleship of Christ, consisting in a renunciation of possessions and active love for one's neighbour. New spiritual communities arose; some, e.g. the Humiliati and the Franciscans, were integrated into the church only after the religious orders. And soon the church began to wage a vigorous war on other radical groups like the Waldensians or the Cathari, who wanted to reform the ministry and the sacraments and were regarded as 'heretics'. Women played a central and active part everywhere. Presumably they had a much more active role among the heretics, because there they had far more chance of participation. But even the communities which were accepted by the church could hardly resist the pressure from women. For example, in five years, between 1246 and 1250, in the Dominican order thirty-two nunneries had to be taken over within the German province.

Many motives prompted the new movements, but the religious unrest among women must also be seen in connection with social causes. Thus, for example, because of the high death rate among males as a result of disease and the crusades, there was a surplus of women. The rise of a monetary economy, the beginnings of industry, the increase in city populations all altered family structures. Moreover, in southern France, where women's movements were very strong and were supported by a large number of noblewomen, changes had been made in the laws of inheritance among the nobility; in order to preserve land-holdings, daughters were barred from inheriting and formed a new class, intent on action.

Thus more women from every class than ever before were thrown back on themselves and sought their own purposes in life. Many travelled with the wandering preachers; others looked for firm ties outside the family.

The church had to cope with the problem of women and the

flood of women who kept presenting themselves, and to look for new practical and ideal solutions. In the course of time, different forms of community life began to develop: there were both the women's communities who lived without any form of monastic order as, for example, the Beguines, and communities which had fixed rules of life, who attached themselves to the new orders. An introverted image of women was now no longer enough. The activities of women called for a new model.

This was the setting for the new image of Martha. There were possibilities of identifying with Martha, because of her orientation on action. The new orders, focussed on action, vied in adopting her. The Humiliati, the Franciscans, smaller brotherhoods, like the Compagnia della Morte, which specialized in caring for those suffering from the plague, made her the patron saint of churches and communities. Furthermore, the Dominican preachers also painted pictures of her, and her name was given to hospitals and homes for widows, which were also adorned with her statue.

A Nuremberg couple who in the course of time founded a church and a pilgrim hospital along with it, called the church after Martha. Almost two hundred years later, the Martha altar was made for it (this is now in the church of St Laurence). Even the Abbot of the monastery of Hirsau, a member of the old and traditional order of Benedictines, in his delight for reform seems to have prompted the Magdalene altar of Tiefenbronn and to have given the painter theological advice: there Martha has attained a new status alongside her sister. At a later date, Ignatius Loyola, the founder of the Jesuit order, is said to have held her in special veneration. Thus Martha was not the saint of a particular order, but for a great variety of groups became the image of revolution aimed at new responsible action in the world.

It is uncertain how far women themselves painted this picture. Artists and abbots were men, and this patriarchal age has given us little information about initiatives taken by women. However, it is certain today that at this time language, imagery and preaching were shaped by women, and that the mysticism of the convents was a decisive influence on the spiritual movement that we call German mysticism.

Was the cult of Martha observed primarily among women? The active women's movement in the south of France and the veneration of Martha which emerged there at the same time suggests as much. It is also striking that Domenicus, the founder of the order of Dominicans, did his decisive work in the south of France, where this legend and tradition about Martha had come into being. He always worked with women, organized their communities and concerned himself with winning women away from heretical circles. Did he discover the new Martha there in women's groups, and is it mere coincidence that the Dominicans were the ones who cherished their own special image of Martha, directed against the tradition?

We know from Meister Eckhart to what extent his sermons and his patterns of thinking are derived from the stimuli which he received from convents, and how he was in constant communication with these convents. His reverent amazement at Martha was presumably kindled by a woman, and his warning against the all-too-convenient enjoyment shown by Mary similarly reflects the experiences of nuns in a convent. We are now becoming aware that many works of art presented in the name of male artists were in fact created by women. Was this sermon about women perhaps also written by a woman? Be this as it may, the new Martha met the needs of women who dissociated themselves from the old orders and looked for a new self-understanding.

Who was this Martha? What did she mean to the new women's movement? What opportunities did she offer to the woman of the late mediaeval period? In addition to Meister Eckhart's revolutionary interpretation, it is the works of art which above all give us some clue.

First of all Martha must be seen distinct from, or even in contrast to, Mary. In the early Middle Ages legends had gathered around the two figures: first around Mary who, as we shall discover in due course, was identified with Mary Magdalene, and later also around Martha. According to legend they were two sisters from Bethany; with Lazarus they were expelled from Palestine, put on a raft, and in this way arrived in France. Here all three became involved in missionary work. In the earlier legend about Mary Magdalene, Martha was still completely overshadowed by her more racy, more attractive sister; later, however, a Martha legend developed, and we shall consider this in detail. Meister Eckhart, who refers back to the earlier, Mary Magdalene legend, dissociates himself from the chief heroine and prefers Martha. Other contemporaries were not quite so radical and set up the two types of woman side by side. However, the image of Martha increasingly took on substance. Martha became an independent figure, acquired character and colour, and from this point on stole the limelight from Mary.

The art of the fourteenth and fifteenth centuries is full of praise of the competent, spiritual Martha: in a side chapel in the Church of Santa Croce in Florence, Giovanni di Milano depicted her as the host at Bethany, illuminated, as it were, by an inner light (1336). In St Martha's Church in Lugano (fourteenth century), she has the spiritual status of a guardian Madonna, and consecrates the brothers of the order who kneel at her feet. In a picture in the monastery in Foligno she sits by the fire weary, but suffused with gratitude and caught up in the spirit (fifteenth century). In Tiefenbronn, near Pforzheim, where the altar (1431) portrays the dramatic story of the sisters from Bethany, from their voyage on a drifting raft to their experiences in Marseilles, she stands alongside Lazarus, now made a bishop, in beautiful tranquillity and spiritual sovereignty. There is no longer any trace of the common earthiness which the church fathers attributed to her, or of later scenes in

THE WOMEN AROUND JESUS

the kitchen and the modern picture of Martha, the faithful servant. She has taken on her own features over against Lazarus and Mary. Her face is always turned directly towards the on-looker. She emanates rest and security. Whereas Mary, bowed down in a position of penitence, is anointing Jesus' feet, Martha is serving the food. Whereas Mary, on the perilous raft, is discussing vigorously with the men, Martha is rapt in prayer. Whereas Lazarus, exhausted after the arrival in Marseilles, has fallen asleep on her lap and has taken off all his episcopal insignia apart from his mitre, Martha has wrapped him in his bishop's cloak, like a mother nursing her baby. Her activity is immaculate, her spirituality indubitable. Martha is the quiet, tranquil centre in contrast to the over-dramatized Mary Magdalene and the men, who seem somewhat ridiculous and almost superfluous. Lastly, on the pedestal of the altar the painter Lucas Moser depicted her as a wise virgin and Mary Magdalene as a foolish virgin. This was a reversal of all previous values. In this way Martha became the woman who attained new recognition and a new sense of her own worth.

In comparison with the less stable, more agitated, young Mary Magdalene, Martha is the mature older women. Though her sister had been made the embodiment of the lusts of the flesh, of seduced and seductive sexuality, and had thus become involved in a portrayal of the beautiful but dangerous woman, thought up by men and encouraged by the church, Martha is free of such conflicts. Her beauty is the beauty of maturity. In the whole of her existence she is at one with the will of God. She is *totally* accepted. She is a good tree which brings forth good fruits. This causes fewer tensions among males. It may be tedious and unexciting. Presumably these portrayals of Martha in art and imagery were supported more strongly by women than we can demonstrate today.

In comparison with Magdalene the 'great sinner' (*magna peccatrix*), Martha emerged as the 'great mother' (*magna mater*). Many images of the Madonna from the same period show the

MARTHA

same ancient matriarchal elements as appear in connection with Martha, and which had at times been suppressed by patriarchal Christian conceptions. There is, for example, the outspread cloak under which the Madonna shelters her own, whether these be monks, churches or children. The masculine images of God and his Son in Christianity had continually suppressed vital elements of femininity. Now in the late Middle Ages it was again possible for all the basic matriarchal needs to be fulfilled. We frequently find dominant figures of wives and mothers with whom the masculine element has become a child. Although, as Erich Neumann thinks, the mother culture may at the same time have found a home among the heresies, at least in the cult of Martha we find an expression of people's wishes for an awareness among women of their femininity, for sovereign motherhood, and for the integrative sagacity and wisdom of the woman. The Martha of this period often has a vessel in her hand. This is the famous jar of oil, which did not really go with her but with her sister, who was thought to have anointed Jesus. However, the jar of oil has become a vessel, a symbol, of the woman. Her body is a vessel. Her implements are vessels. Martha, the *magna mater*, becomes the embodiment of the mature, powerful, creative woman who fulfils herself and makes her own contribution, who calls forth the wonderment of the male.

The Dominican painter Fra Angelico has left us a picture of Martha which is probably unique in the history of art. In the fine Dominican tradition he continued to develop the Martha story imaginatively in the monastery of San Marco in Florence: this time the scene is Gethsemane. In the background Jesus is praying that the cup of crucifixion may pass from him, and an angel is hovering below and strengthening him. Left of centre, Peter, James and John are enjoying sweet and blessed sleep, overcome by their helplessness. To the right, in the foreground, Martha and Mary are sitting awake, keeping watch – protected by a house wall. The haloes with their names single them out.

Mary's head is bowed and she is reading a book. Martha is fully alert, casting questioning looks at Mary and praying with uplifted hands, adopting the same attitude as the sorely tried Jesus in the background. Contemplation and action, the characteristics of the two sisters, are still recognizable. However, the action of Martha is now a readiness to watch with Jesus which has grown from her own total involvement, her own spirituality. The disciples are the ones who fail, who fall asleep. Here Fra Angelico has taken up the old story, to be found in Matthew and Mark, of the disciples who fail and the women who see things through to the end. But in no other instance does a painter seem to have taken Martha from the idyll of Bethany and shown her perseverance in the darkest hour of human failure in Gethsemane.

Martha is very near to Jesus, in her discipleship, in her attitide. She, the woman, is the real disciple of Jesus.

Fra Angelico interpreted the biblical tradition in accordance with his picture of Martha in yet another painting. He represents her as the only woman alongside St Veronica beneath the cross. Again it is her hands which she uses, actively and in prayer, at the same time raising them in entreaty towards the crucified Jesus.

Perhaps she is also meant to be portrayed in yet a third picture. She is wearing the same green cloak as in the other two pictures. The dead Jesus is laid in the tomb. Mary, his mother, is settling his head, Mary Magdalene his feet, which she has anointed, while the figure in the green cloak is holding his hand firmly in her own.

A very ancient apocryphal gospel has Mary and Martha present at the crucifixion. Did Fra Angelico know it?

There were enough other women who are shown to have been present at the crucifixion, at the death of Jesus and at his burial, and who could have provided the material. The fact that Martha takes their place or appears alongside them is a sign of the symbolic force of her figure in the religious revolution of the Middle Ages.

(ii) Martha defeating the dragon

Another mediaeval image of Martha, which shows the revolution that took place among mediaeval women, and still deeper levels of consciousness, is that of Martha defeating the dragon.

Even experts in Christian art are hardly aware of such pictures. However, the observant onlooker will continually come across paintings, statues or church windows which depict Martha with a dragon at her feet: south of the Main, in southern Switzerland, in France and in Italy. This theme was attractive above all to the painters of the Renaissance, who rediscovered woman and, with her, nature and the earth in all their beauty. The best-known paintings are by such famous artists as Berhardino Luini, Antonio Corregio and Bartholomew Zeitblom. Hardly any of the late mediaeval painters could avoid this fascinating and popular theme. The pictures are so varied and so widespread that no iconography has yet succeeded in embracing all these representations of Martha. The first images appear in southern France in the fourteenth century, and during the fifteenth and sixteenth centuries spread to northern Italy and southern Germany. Remarkably, they appear in those parts of Italy to which the sect of the Cathari was driven by the Inquisition, in Tuscany and Lombardy. Did Martha correspond to their independent image of women? Does she even derive from their circles?

Martha defeating the dragon now no longer recalls the housewife in Luke who is reprimanded by Jesus. Martha does not just exude tranquillity and superiority: she is proud, confident of victory, self-assured. She is often depicted as a mature woman, sometimes as a nun, but also as an elegant young society lady. In a cheerful baroque church in Ticino, decorated all over with angels, she is like a radiant Greek goddess in a

A man defeats the dragon

St George Fountain, Tübingen.
In the background is a window of the Stiftskirche depicting the
fight with the dragon.

A woman defeats the dragon

Martha.
Pilgrimage Church of Madonna d'Ongero in Carona, near
Lugano. First half of the eighteenth century.

white garment. In one hand she usually holds a pitcher and a holy water sprinkler or a cross, with which she has bound the dragon. In the other hand she is holding her girdle, the symbol of purity, with which she has fettered him.

Her proud certainty of victory is now in abrupt contrast to the teeth-gnashing monster at her feet. Here the imagination of the artist has found a rich sphere of activity: the dragon is a monstrous serpent. It looks like an armoured dinosaur, and walks on lion's feet or fins. With all its overpowering might, it rolls at Martha's feet. It peers craftily and furtively at its conqueror. Like a fairy-tale animal, it has wings, which droop sadly in defeat. We can still see how terrible it is, since it is not dead but only captured, conquered, made harmless, bound. On the Martha altar at Nuremberg the dragon's victim can still be half-seen: a man with a tunic and bare feet. Will the dragon free him again? All the biblical beasts which symbolize evil are united in the dragon: the serpent, the apocalyptic dragon, the beast from the abyss.

Even where the victory over the dragon has not become a theme, in a number of representations of Martha the dragon is still there in the background: on a reliquary in the sanctuary shrine in Halle he has been reduced to a toy figure in her hand. Tiny dragon imps are painted on the background of green clouds against which the Martha of the Tiefenbronn altar is set.

What is the origin of this mythological tradition about Martha, which we find strange, and which has almost been forgotten?

The Middle Ages are rich in legends which told of the further course of the lives of biblical figures and embroidered them in an imaginative way where the biblical narrative seemed to be too bare and terse. These were intertwined with episodes from the early church and the experiences of well-known Christians, often giving rise to a remarkable mixture of flowery fantasy, archaic human truth and biblical themes. The south of France provided particularly fruitful soil for this. As I shall show in due

42

course, there developed here above all a cult of Mary Magdalene, and in its wake a cult of Lazarus and Martha, each connected with a particular place and each with traditions of their own. Mary Magdalene was revered above all in Vezelay and later in St Baume, Lazarus in Autun, and Martha in Tarascon. The story which they share tells how the three from Bethany were expelled from Palestine. With many other Christians they were put on a boat by the unbelievers and sent to sea without a rudder, 'so that they would all perish'. The pictures on the altar at Tiefenbronn give a vivid portrayal of this voyage in the rudderless vessel, the arrival of the three kinsfolk in Marseilles, and the beginning of the missionary activity of Mary Magdalene.

In this cycle of stories, which principally clusters around Mary Magdalene, Martha has a secondary role. However, an independent Martha tradition soon came into being. Martha was already receiving veneration for herself alone in southern France in the tenth century. A church in Tarascon was named after her in the eleventh century. In 1187 there were claims that her relics had been discovered there, and ten years later a new church was built and dedicated to her.

The Martha legend proper developed apparently independently, but not without connections with this situation. According to this, following the ideals of the time, Martha led an ascetic life – she was a vegetarian – and was in charge of a convent. However – and now she proves a more rebellious figure – she preached, healed the sick and raised a dead person who had wanted to listen to her preaching, swam across a river and was drowned. Martha's apostolic function had been rediscovered! But there was even more: legend transferred to her a traditional masculine role, victory over the dragon.

The inhabitants of the countryside between Arles and Avignon asked for her help. A man-eating dragon, called Tarascus, 'half animal and half fish', fatter than an ox and longer than a horse, with teeth like swords and pointed like horns, lay submerged in the Rhone and killed anyone who tried to cross, sinking their ships. 'St Martha went out against the dragon, because the people asked her to. She found him in the forest, eating a man. Immediately she sprinkled holy water on him and set a cross before him; thereupon he was conquered and stood like a tame lamb. Martha bound him with her girdle. After that the people came and killed him with stones and spears.'

The enlightened twentieth-century Protestant may laugh at this Christianized dragon story and regard it as a relapse into mythological prehistory. However, it is worth noting for a number of reasons: biblical, cultural and psychological. The theme of a sea or land monster who threatens the inhabitants of a city is known in the mythology of almost all peoples. Usually the monster requires a sacrifice, often a pure virgin, until the hero comes, frees the victim and conquers the monstrous dragon. Thus in Greek legend Heracles rescues Hesione. In the same way, when Greek mythology has been translated into Christian mythology, St George frees Margaret, the princess chosen to be the dragon's victim, and slays the dragon. (Margaret is similarly portrayed with the fettered dragon bound by her girdle. However, she belongs in the legend of George, which derives from Asia Minor, and is the victim who is rescued, not the conqueror herself.)

Various elements from the dragon legend recur in the legend of Martha: the dragon threatens a city and people fall victim to it. Like the rescued princess, Martha binds the dragon with her girdle and in this way leads him into the city, where he is killed. The woman's girdle makes the dragon as tame as a lamb or a small dog.

However, in contrast to the canonical legend of the victory over the dragon, here the decisive figure – the rider, the knight, the mighty hero, the soldier – is absent. What has happened?

A single theme from the dragon legend has taken on a life of its own: the woman who was the victim now replaces the male hero. With this, we have a portentous development which is against all the laws of mythology; the woman is confronted with her like. She herself has a close affinity to the dragon and is continually connected with it: Demeter sits on a chariot drawn by dragons; the serpent, 'the old dragon', often has a woman's head – and think of the custom of calling forbidding women 'dragons'. Thus woman is no longer simply the embodiment of disorder and chaos; she is no longer a threat. A woman conquers that which is feared by women. In Christian legend she is on a par with man. The Martha legend transcends an age-old patriarchal symbolism which is built up on the dualism of man and chaos (= woman) and the identification of woman with chaos. The evaluation of women in negative terms, in terms of chaos, is abolished. Patriarchal mythology ends in a biblical, Christian figure.

The difference between the woman's victory over the dragon and that of the man is a striking one. The legend told how George leaped on to his horse, wielded his lance with great power and hit the dragon so hard that he fell to the ground. At the end of the story George draws his sword and kills the dragon. Suppose we compare the pictures of Martha and George. In the masculine version, a man, booted and spurred, thrusts his lance into the dragon's mouth with all his might. In some accounts the lance breaks. The dragon is fatally wounded. In the feminine version the heroine conquers and tames the dragon with vulnerable bare feet and in a flowing robe, using holy water and a sprinkler or a cross. It is the people who kill the monster.

In the masculine version force comes up against counter-force. Martha encounters the dragon without killing it. Martha overcomes the threat without force. She does not need to go to this last resort. Nevertheless, she wins. And she has features of both victor and victim. She has bound the monster with her whole existence and has become the victor. By contrast, a Rumanian saint, Marina, who according to one legend smote the devil with a hammer, is in accord with patriarchal models.

Ideas associated with the dragon extend from the death of the old order, chaos, to heresy and paganism in the Middle Ages. To begin with, the early Martha to be found in the south of France and her victory over the dragon were connected with hope for the conversion of the pagans and victory over the heretics. Martha was a missionary saint. However, it would be too easy here to remain superficial and fail to notice the psychological aspects of the development of patriarchal mythology.

In Greek legend, the victory of the mind, the consciousness, over the unconscious, the primal monster, reflects the victory of a patriarchal culture over primitive matriarchal forms. The hero, who embodied rationality and consciousness, had to be male. The Christian church took up this theme in the story of George, the man who killed the dragon, and identified itself with the patriarchal level of consciousness. 'Any patriarchal world,' writes Erich Neumann, '. . . is based on a concern to banish this titanic element . . . into the primal womb of the underworld. Consequently, the patriarchal world takes pride in representing itself with its foot on the head of the conquering dragon of the deep.' The resurrection of Christ was also interpreted in this way, as Christ trampling down the serpent's head, but nowadays this interpretation has been replaced by another.

By contrast, the Martha legend represents a new development. Now a woman symbolizes the victory over the unconscious, death, the threat, and she has conquered the dragon in a new way. She has not trampled it down, but bound it. Martha marks the symbolic beginning of another way of dealing with evil: not its annihilation but its redemption, 'the transformation of the underside,' as Erich Neumann puts it, though without introducing a symbol for this.

If we go on to recall how many pictures of serpents or dragons from the story of the Fall show the serpent with a woman's face, and to what extent the early church and the early Middle Ages located the primal sin in woman and her sexuality, the picture of Martha and the dragon shows a new way of dealing with woman, with nature, with the senses and with sexuality. Martha, who involves herself in pleading for the raising of Lazarus, the woman who is the first to hear that Jesus is the resurrection and the life, and who confesses this, shows a new way of relating to the natural forces, to death and threats to life. It is significant that the theme of Martha and the dragon reached a climax in the feminist culture of the Renaissance. Here are signs of a new humanism: nature is integrated, and new value is attached to women. Then the Reformation and the Counter Reformation ended almost everywhere the emancipation of Martha, by which she became the victor over the dragon.

The tradition about George and the dragon, which continued its way untroubled in the background, had stronger symbolic force and longer staying-power in a masculine world and a church which was again becoming a masculine sphere of activity. It is an expression of rule over the world, nature, oneself; it is the image of a powerful masculine Christianity. In the Crusades it became the theme of Christian action in a world which was to be conquered and taken in possession, and thus spread up into the lands of the north, where it is celebrated in poetry and imagery even now.

The two symbols could still appear side by side in peaceful co-existence even in the late Middle Ages and down to the baroque period. We find painters who painted both themes, and we know churches which combine Martha and George. The little mountain community of Carona, above Lugano, shows a particularly fine example of a tradition about Martha and George which continued in the mountains of Ticino until the eighteenth century.

The earliest church is the Martha church from the fifteenth century, which has already been mentioned. On great late-Gothic frescoes, a noble patroness Martha – with the well-known girdle around her robe – is consecrating the monks of an order who want to devote themselves to the care of those smitten by the plague. A small image in relief, modest against the background of the church, shows George fighting the dragon. The village church itself is dedicated to the man who conquered the dragon: over the entrance there is a small relief, and inside the church there is a large and vivid picture showing George thrusting his spear into the dragon's jaws, while the rescued princess looks on with folded arms.

A third church, the pilgrimage church of Madonna d'Ongero, in the forest, dating from the second half of the eighteenth century, has combined the two themes: at the front of the nave is a proud, baroque Martha, conquering the dragon, and there is a smaller relief of George in the entrance.

This latest testimony to the Martha tradition once again maintains the matriarchal Martha cult of the Middle Ages, with its propensity towards women. However, the patriarchal tradition of Christian culture was stronger: today the tradition of Martha and the dragon has been forgotten. George became the key symbol of the *militia Christi*, and would not tolerate feminine counterparts and alternative life-styles, as in the Middle Ages. The patriarchal symbols of George or Siegfried have shaped us and our world, and like the princess in the legend of George and the dragon, women remain objects to be freed. Today, where feminine patterns of behaviour and alternative life-styles are again coming into prominence, the Martha symbol is taking on new powers of expression.

A woman anoints the
feet of Jesus

*The Anointing at
Bethany.
Painting on wood. An
altar wing by Nicolaus
Froment, Uffizi Gallery,
Florence, 1461.*

2

MARY OF BETHANY

Mary sat down at the feet of the Lord and listened to his teaching (Luke 10.39).

Jesus loved Martha and her sister Mary and Lazarus . . . Martha called her sister privately. 'The Teacher is here,' she told her, 'and is asking for you.' When Mary heard this, she got up and hurried out to meet him. (Jesus had not yet arrived in the village, but was still in the place where Martha had met him.) The people who were in the house with Mary, comforting her, followed her when they saw her get up and hurry out. They thought that she was going to the grave to weep there. Mary arrived where Jesus was, and as soon as she saw him, she fell at his feet. 'Lord,' she said, 'if you had been here my brother would not have died!' Jesus saw her weeping, and he saw how the people who were with her were weeping also; his heart was touched, and he was deeply moved (John 11.5, 28–33).

Six days before the Passover Jesus went to Bethany, the home of Lazarus, the man he had raised from the dead. They prepared a dinner for him there, which Martha helped to serve. Lazarus was one of those who were sitting at the table with Jesus. Then Mary took half a litre of a very expensive perfume made of pure nard, poured it on Jesus' feet and wiped them with her hair. The sweet smell of the perfume filled the house. One of Jesus' disciples, Judas Iscariot – the one who was going to betray him – said, 'Why wasn't this perfume sold for three hundred silver coins and the money given to the poor?' He said this, not because he cared about the poor, but because he was a thief. He carried the money bag and would help himself from it. But Jesus said, 'Leave her alone! Let her keep what she has for the day of my burial. You will always have poor people with you, but you will not always have me' (John 12.1–8).

Mary is quiet and comes to Jesus only when she is expressly called. As the context shows, her feelings are deeper than those of Martha. She falls down before Jesus; she does not say much, but in so doing she manages to convey a profound impression of her grief (Johannes Leipoldt).

It is the contemplative who is drawn to Jesus, and precisely at this point we find the new element in the relationship between Jesus and the women around him (Shalom Ben Chorim).

Every housewife should follow Mary's example and for a while free herself to be open to new spiritual impulses. According to Christ's will, too, she must also be more to her husband than a mere housekeeper and more to her children than a provider . . . Sometimes she must rest from work, sit down and listen patiently and caringly to her children or her husband, when they want to discuss their joys or their pains with her (Peter Ketter).

We suspect that dear Mary sits there more out of pleasure than for her spiritual advancement. That is why Martha says, 'Lord, make her get up!', because she is afraid that Mary might continue in this delight and not advance in any way (Meister Eckhart).

In Mary, then, we find a portrayal of the first stage of faith, beyond which her sister had advanced . . . Mary does not have Martha's certainty (Rudolf Bultmann)

MARY OF BETHANY

In the shadow of her sister

Mary of Bethany suffers the fate of many women: her voice is not loud, what she says is not original, her story is not dramatic. Her behaviour is not noticeable, her conduct is modest. She seems sympathetic, but by the next time people have forgotten her name and confuse her with another woman who has made more of an impression.

The common Jewish name Mary has itself contributed to this. There are six Maries in the New Testament alone: the mother of two disciples; a Christian in Rome; the mother of John Mark, at whose home the early church meets; Mary of Bethany; and lastly the two most famous Maries: the mother of Jesus and Mary of Magdala, who is known under the name of Mary Magdalene. The shadow of the latter has almost overwhelmed Mary of Bethany. Because John recorded that Mary of Bethany had anointed the feet of Jesus and a similar anointing story was told of a prostitute who was quite wrongly – connected with Mary Magdalene, the two figures were fused. So Martha got a sister who was often taken to be Mary Magdalene. This mistake has been common from the Middle Ages down to the present day. Graphic artists, poets and even theologians have fallen victim to it, and the débris of so many errors has disfigured Mary's appearance. Painters portrayed Martha and Mary Magdalene as sisters. This stereotyped pair of sisters appeared again in legends. Even the modern memoirs of Jesus written by the theologian Jean Claude Barreau revived this convenient error. It is easier to understand and portray stereotyped women.

Thus it was difficult for Mary of Bethany to lead a life of her own. She does not fare much better in the New Testament stories in which she appears. In Luke's story of the visit of Jesus to Mary and Martha at Bethany (Luke 10) she sits at Jesus' feet to listen to him. In John's story of the raising of Lazarus

(John 11) she remains with the guests who come to mourn the death of her brother. Thus both times she has to put up with the sharp comments of her sister Martha, who thinks that she is tame and passive. 'The Teacher is here and is asking for you,' she tells Mary, to stir her up a bit. And she complains to Jesus that Mary leaves her to do all the work. Along with his comp^tent contemporaries, the active orders of nuns, Meister Eckhart suspected that 'dear Mary' was sitting there more out of pleasure than for spiritual advancement. Impressive remarks by the eloquent and hasty Martha have come down to us. From Mary we have only one sentence, which Martha had already uttered: 'Lord, if you had been here, my brother would not have died.' Otherwise there is nothing but tears, falling down at Jesus' feet, sitting at Jesus' feet, anointing his feet. Many women today find this kind of behaviour offensive rather than attractive.

Now it is remarkable how this Mary – independent, dear, not talking back when her sister attacks her, with tears in her eyes and always ready to efface herself, has aroused the sympathy of theologians. In Peter Ketter's phrase, she is a 'quiet, tranquil soul', who is so dear to the heart of preaching theologians, in complete contrast to the self-confident and eloquent Martha. Thus one commentator, Hirsch, thinks that in the silent, worshipful Mary John wanted to depict the 'Christian attitude towards suffering and death'. The New Testament scholar Leipoldt, concerned with the role of women, is enthusiastic about the quiet Mary who comes to Jesus only when she is expressly called, and who has 'deeper feelings' than the overloud Martha. And the Jewish writer Shalom Ben Chorim ends the feminine ideal which has extended from Luke and the time of the church fathers down the present day when he writes, 'It is the contemplative to whom Jesus is drawn, and precisely at this point we find the new element in the relationship between Jesus and the women around him.' Mary, the contemplative life, the secret feminine ideal of all times, is today the ideal of alternative life-styles. In the full light of day, however, this is more a philosophical and Stoic dream than a Christian one.

To be gentle, to be lovely, to be able to fall on one's knees is not necessarily a sign of strong faith. The New Testament, and above all John's story of the raising of Lazarus, has made this plain. Rudolf Bultmann, at any rate, has seen clearly that John wanted to use Mary to depict the first stage of faith. 'She does not have Martha's certainty.' But now John goes on to tell a third story of Martha and Mary, almost to make good the previous story, and this is a story about Mary alone: the anointing of Jesus by Mary in Bethany (John 12). This time Martha is manifestly in the background. There is a supper. Martha is serving, and now Mary is the protagonist. Again she is not helping, but what she does comes from the very depths of her personality.

She takes a flask of very expensive perfume and pours it over the feet of Jesus who is reclining beside her on the cushions round the table. She may not be good at words, but what she does without speaking and yet with great self-confidence has a spontaneous effect: the whole house becomes filled with the fragrance. The sweetness of her action is evident everywhere. This time she did not have Martha to urge her on – not that that ever had any effect! This time she is completely herself, and in so doing transcends herself. All the elemental ways in which she was accustomed to express her spontaneous love for Jesus, her respect, her affection, her tenderness – the tears, the concern to be near him and to have his support, the spontaneous silence – are now released with the fragrant oil with which she refreshes the tired and dusty feet of her friend. And even that is not enough: with her hair she wipes away the dust and oil from his feet and dries them. That was the task of the lowliest slave: the master at the table used to wipe his dirty hands on the slave's hair.

Mary performs this servile task in a way which is incomprehensible to many women today. She does what no man would

55

have done – it would be inconceivable even to Martha. Self-debasement? Self-defilement? But what she does, she does of her own accord and in the light of her personality. It is *her* idea, *her* way of showing love. It is her 'revolution'.

This time she is not led on by her sister. Perhaps Martha stood there transfixed and dumbfounded at such independence. Mary had broken out of the ghetto in which she had been held captive. She came out of the shadows to become totally herself: the clumsy, loving, independent, tender, restrained and yet spontaneous woman.

Provocation

Anyone who becomes a personality is provocative, and gains enemies. The enemy here is not a Pharisee, as in the anointing of the woman who was a great sinner (Luke), nor the crowd as a whole, as at the anointing by an unknown woman (Mark). It is one of the influential disciples: Judas, who looks after the finances of the group. When Jesus visited the sisters, Mary provoked Martha by her modest but impressive attitude. Now she does the same thing to the powerful Judas. The spendthrift and eccentric attitude of so unlikely a woman arouses his social wrath: think of all the poor people who could have been fed and clothed! But as on the former occasion, when Martha wanted to force Mary into the kitchen, Jesus comes to protect her. 'Leave her alone!' As then, he takes her as she is and interprets her extravagant eccentricity as love which will go with him to his death.

John attributed the anointing of Jesus by a woman, a happening well known in the earliest community, to the inconspicuous and quiet Mary. As we shall see later, the story is told in different ways and of different women. This was not any old story. It was *the* loving action of a woman which people always wanted to mention when they talked about Jesus. And John sees Mary in this important role.

56

He goes on to place his own special emphasis on it: the action proves provocative, not to a disturbed gathering and a Pharisee, but to the notorious Judas. Mary's generosity is set off against his avarice, his pettiness against her large-heartedness. The contemplative woman beloved of males shows highly inconvenient, indeed unattractive features to a world which has a pragmatic orientation. Here Luke and John have discovered roughly the same thing about Mary: the woman who is restrained because of the ways of behaving in society which have been instilled into her, is beginning a voiceless but nevertheless impressive revolution. The difference between the two narrators lies in the fact that Luke attributes this to the vital Martha, while John lets the two figures be involved side by side.

John's Mary story is the story of a woman who becomes herself. Even in the Lazarus story she remains in the crowd, does not detach herself from it and does not hear Jesus' voice; she therefore is not one of his, has not yet been grasped by him and has not become independent (John 10.3f.).

But then she discovers how she can offer herself, *her* faith, *her* love. If Martha has felt the reality of the resurrection, Mary experiences the nearness of Jesus to death, the danger, the anguish which she herself feels in many little anxieties. There is something of her story in the story of Jesus. That makes her free, untroubled and capable of action. She is still tongue-tied. She still seems to be attractive and capable of fitting in with others. But she has become herself and is doing something which no one else has done, even the hasty Martha. In doing what she does, she provokes conflict, even with a man, which one would never have expected from her. She is no longer overshadowed by Martha, but at the same time she is no longer under Martha's protection. She lives in an unprecedented independence which she has learned through Jesus. A woman is freed from innate and inculcated patterns of behaviour. She learns to be herself, or, as Meister Eckhart puts it, she learns to live.

Mary, man's quiet dream, is also dynamite: the revolutionary potential of love, which we keep wanting to reduce to the small and modest love of women, so that the calculating world remains undisturbed. Mary has a face of her own, the face of many women. But she begins a history of her own which has no parallels, except perhaps in the history of women who discover that the gospel does not suppress their individuality but develops it, and amounts to the adventure of being themselves.

Mary Magdalene, beautiful and seductive . . .

Mary Magdalene.
Painting by a pupil of Caravaggio. Late Middle Ages.

3

MARY MAGDALENE

After Jesus rose from death early on Sunday, he appeared first to Mary Magdalene, from whom he had driven out seven demons. She went and told his companions. They were mourning and crying; and when they heard her say that Jesus was alive and that she had seen him, they did not believe her (Mark 16.9–11).

Mary stood crying outside the tomb. While she was still crying, she bent over and looked in the tomb and saw two angels there dressed in white, sitting where the body of Jesus had been, one at the head and the other at the feet. 'Woman, why are you crying?' they asked her. She answered, 'They have taken my Lord away, and I do not know where they have put him!'
Then she turned round and saw Jesus standing there; but she did not know that it was Jesus. 'Woman, why are you crying?' Jesus asked her. 'Who is it that you are looking for?' She thought he was the gardener, so she said to him, 'If you took him away, sir, tell me where you have put him, and I will go and get him.' Jesus said to her, 'Mary!' She turned towards him and said in Hebrew, 'Rabboni!' (This means 'Teacher'.) 'Do not hold on to me,' Jesus told her, 'because I have not yet gone back up to the Father. But go to my brothers and tell them that I am returning to him who is my Father and their Father, my God and their God.' So Mary Magdalene went and told the disciples that she had seen the Lord and related to them what he had told her (John 20.11–18)

. . . and the 'Sinner'
who repents

Mary Magdalene as
the Great Penitent.
Donatello, Baptistery
of S. Giovanni,
Florence.

MARY MAGDALENE

Jesus,
I imagine
how you must have loved Mary Magdalene,
who was beautiful,
and smelled of flowers.
When you put your arms round her,
her surrender
was as great
as a divine love (Ernst Eggimann).

Mary the *hetaira*, Mary Magdalene, that is, Miriam from the west bank of Lake Gennesaret, from whom Jesus is said to have driven out seven evil spirits, which people at a later date were fond of connecting with the seven deadly sins, is the prototype of the sinner whom Jesus accepts into his circle (Shalom Ben Chorin).

'Care of those in danger'
This term originally embraced care for those who were in some danger on grounds of morality, health or occupation; from the middle of the 1920s it has been used in a narrower sense for the work of accepting those in sexual danger, primarily endangered women and young girls (earlier known as 'Magdalene Care'). This work is the prime sphere of Christian charity. Care for those in danger already began in the Middle Ages in the order of Penitents of St Mary Magdalene (the thirteenth-century Magdalene Convent) . . . On the Protestant side the basis for a comprehensive care for those in danger was only laid by Fliedner and in particular by the Dutch pastor Heldring. Heldring's principles were freedom to come and go; as a means of education he made use of daily prayer, work which would serve as training in household duties to meet the conditions, capabilities and later progress of those concerned, like washing, sewing, ironing, helping in the kitchen and garden, and so on,

and in addition to this, loving pastoral concern. A large number of Magdalene hostels have been formed in Germany, following this pattern . . . (*Calwer Kirchenlexikon*, 1937).

'Would the Redeemer, then, have spoken secretly with a woman without letting us know? Should we perhaps repent and all listen to her? Has he preferred her to us?' (Peter, about Mary Magdalene in the apocryphal *Gospel according to Mary Magdalene*).

The Holy Spirit made Magdalene the apostle of the apostles (Augustine).

A 'great sinner'?

Anyone who loves the biblical Mary Magdalene, and compares her with the 'Christian' Mary Magdalene, must get very angry. And to begin with, I must give vent to this anger here.

Even now, for most people Mary Magdalene is the 'great sinner'. Literature and art in the Western tradition, stories and pictures of the repentant and penitent woman whose past beauty can still be seen, have stamped our picture of Mary Magdalene. Even Protestant theologians who, following the custom of the Reformation, want to understand themselves only in terms of the Word and the Bible, still fall victim to this error. But the great sinner, of whom Luke speaks (Luke 7), and Mary Magdalene, whom all four Gospels report, have as little to do with each other as Peter and Judas. What has been done to Mary Magdalene in the history of the Western church corresponds to the fatal Christian identification of Judas and Jews. Just as in the latter case an individual and his fate become the prototype of a whole people, who are then regarded with hatred and anger, so in the former, sexual sin is projected on to a young woman who then bears this charge on behalf of the whole female sex. And just as in the former case there is need for clarification and a disclosure of sub-conscious presuppositions, so Mary Magdalene must again become the woman with her own personal history, rather than being the prototype of the sinful woman.

How did this fateful development begin?

According to the biblical narratives, Mary Magdalene was the woman who stood closest to Jesus. Mary, the mother of Jesus, in no way played this role, which was ascribed to her later. She regarded her son as a frivolous character (Mark 3.21) whom she would really have liked to have taken in hand. The early church always found it a source of great grief that Mary thought so little of the Jesus movement. The fact was hushed up, played down, and finally the evangelist John placed her under the cross. Perhaps this is a hint at her late understanding of the unusual course taken by her son. Luke, too, is aware of the belated recognition of Jesus by his family, and their role in the primitive community (Acts 1.14). However, the woman who stood by Jesus throughout his life, sensitive and understanding, was Mary Magdalene.

She bore the common name Mary, which so many Jewish women had because it was modern and a queen Mary, Herod's first wife, made it fashionable. This trend had the sorry consequence that church fathers, popes, bishops and, following them, artists and writers, could throw all the Maries into the stock pot and take out again and present an appropriate selection from them in accordance with their needs. The spice for this was provided by the story of the woman who was a great sinner, which precedes that of Mary Magdalene's call. Since then the church has tormented women of all ages with the view that they are sinful like Maries and of doubtful piety.

Let us take apart the traditions, which are mixed up with one another like a tangled skein. Luke records the call and healing of Mary Magdalene (ch. 8). The 'evil spirits' indicate a mental illness, perhaps manic depressions or epilepsy. In the previous chapter he tells of the well-known prostitute who forces her way into the Pharisee's house, disturbs the gathering and draws attention to herself, bursts into tears at Jesus' feet and then anoints them. For the church, strict on morality and concerned with its moral purity, feeling that it had to draw the line against pagan sensuality and immorality, nothing was more obvious than to identify the 'evil spirits' with the evil sins of sexuality. In this way the mentally ill woman who was healed became the sexual sinner who showed so vividly in her person to what unrestrained sexuality can lead: to mental disturbance. This is a theory which has caused a great deal of disaster in medicine right down to our own times and has no basis in fact. Thus the two successive chapters in Luke became entangled in a fateful way.

At the same time the different stories about the anointing of Jesus told in Mark 14 and John 12 were confused with Luke's story of the anointing of Jesus by the woman who was a great sinner. Mark does not give the woman any name in his story: the woman who anoints Jesus remains unknown. According to John, it was Mary of Bethany, the sister of Martha and Lazarus, who anointed Jesus. So in the tradition the name of Mary was retained for the woman who anointed Jesus; it was concluded that she and Mary Magdalene the great sinner were one and the same person. The story of the unknown was suppressed, and the woman who anointed Jesus was given the surname Magdalene. The scintillating, moving and dangerous feminine image was complete: Mary Magdalene, the friend of Jesus, who had been a prostitute, the sister of the active Martha of Bethany.

At the expense of women, a provocative imaginary picture had been created in the patriarchal church. What is left of the great male sinner? Did he not exist, just as down to the present century there was a double morality for the diaconate which approved of the punishment of the prostitute but judged the man by a different standard? Biblical men have a past, as fishermen and tax-collectors. *The* figure of biblical womanhood has the past of a 'sinner'.

As I shall demonstrate below, the portrait of Magdalene was constructed by men, and served to kindle male fantasies. It provides a spine-chilling picture of a wasted life, as is expressed in Donatello's statue of the penitent wasted away to a skeleton and worn down by care. At the same time it is a dream of love: sex, eros and agape. Sexual guilt complexes are projected on to Mary Magdalene, and moral demands are connected with her example. In mysticism she was the bride of Christ, and in morality the fallen maiden, and this traditional picture has been taken over unquestioningly, right down to the theological literature of the present. It has been loved, cherished and handed down further in the predominantly masculine production of theological literature.

Mary Magdalene has now changed her image: according to Shalom Ben Chorim, the prostitute of former times has become the *hetaira*, the concubine. She is no longer the adulteress of prudish Victorian times. Rather, to use Strunk's phrase, she is seen in the exalted context of the 'Attis cult', in this 'atmosphere of incense, prostitution and lawlessness'. Moral demands have been liberalized. But the projection of one's own inadequacy and danger on to a weaker, dumber, more helpless counterpart remains the same.

Women in the church have had to identify themselves with this Mary Magdalene who has been handed down to them in sermons and in paintings. They have submitted, just as they have submitted to the masculine portrayal of sin as consisting of pride, sensuality and sexuality, and have internalized it. What would our tradition look like if it had made Peter a converted pimp?

Since women have begun to ask about themselves and their role in the church, the images and conceptions forced upon them have become more and more questionable. Who was the Mary Magdalene of whom the Bible tells? What visions does her story produce among women today? Where is she, our prostitute sister against whom there is so much discrimination?

The biblical Mary Magdalene

Mary Magdalene was really called just 'Mary'; her surname comes from her home town of Magdala, a commercial town on Lake Gennesaret. Trade flourished there. A large fishing fleet and the work that went with it provided a livelihood for the inhabitants and brought prosperity and variety. However, for anyone who lives life under black veils, who suffers from mental disturbances, attacks and depressions, such a place stands in tormenting contrast to experienced reality.

Mary Magdalene suffered from a serious mental illness and was one of those women who came to follow Jesus as a result of her cure.

We may imagine that this cure took a similar course to other healings: Jesus touched her, perhaps embraced her, made her get up, like Peter's feverish mother-in-law or the person possessed by demons. He spoke to her and she had a tangible feeling of nearness and contact. As he spoke, the spell left her. She again became herself, free to feel and decide, free once again to experience the world around her, free to enjoy herself and to learn to live again. But she did not return to her old ways. She left her rich home town of Magdala, even though she would always bear its name.

For her, being healed of her illness became salvation. She felt salvation, very clearly indeed. The two things became fused together. And the group around Jesus could feel this well-being; it shared in her happiness.

The men who were snatched away from a profession and then began their wandering existence were not like this. We do not hear of any healing of a male disciple which was a call. Luke also tells of other women who were healed and who followed Jesus, and Mark describes the healing of Peter's mother-in-law, who as a result 'serves' Jesus, i.e. adopts his style of life. Discipleship affects the whole of these women's existence. They surrender themselves completely, give themselves up completely to the new way of life.

Mary Magdalene is similarly said to have 'served'. Just as Jesus served her, now she too serves him. We shall see in due course how little the serving of the first group of women has to do with modern feminine 'serving', as specifically associated with their sex. To understand Mary Magdalene we must see for ourselves how closely this was connected with mutual and interchangeable physical contacts, human nearness, bodily warmth and healing presence. More intensively than the great unknown woman in Mark (see below) or the Mary of Bethany who anointed Jesus, she lived on the physical proximity of the Jesus community.

In male fantasies she usually seems to be unmarried, young and beautiful. But perhaps she was already aged, had a marriage behind her which provided the means with which she was able to help the Jesus movement, and showed traces of the illness which she had overcome. We do not know. In any case, she must have had charm, warmth and an understanding of people, whether her attraction was that of a mature or a young woman. How else could she have brought together a group of independent women of different ages, separated from their families? All four Gospels always mention her name in first place when they speak of the group of women. So we can assume that she played a leading role and had an integrating effect. We can easily understand how much conflict there must have been among the women who had given up their family ties, between the group of men and the group of women, and not least with the world around, which must have found such women provocative.

Mary Magdalene had the qualities of a leader, and according to Luke (8.3) she contributed wealth. Like Joanna, she helped to bring an urban element to the middle-class Jesus movement. The Jewish women – for the first time without the protection of the wider family – were submissive to her. She was eloquent and persuasive. She could speak, and did not find it difficult to exert her authority. In the later Gospels we can detect this mature sovereignty which always foxed the disciples, especially Peter.

We hear no more of her between her healing and the crucifixion of Jesus. Perhaps her weakened body gained strength during her travels. Certainly she lived on her enthusiasm and the firm conviction that the time of salvation had begun, and all the disappointments which began to trouble the disciples went by her. The Gospels, which in other respects differ over their favourite heroines, agree in reporting that she stood with the women beneath the cross, was present at the burial of Jesus, and was first to go to the tomb on Easter morning.

And this is where her special relationship with Jesus begins. Within the privileged group of women she had yet one more privileged position: the risen Jesus appeared to her and gave her the task of reporting his appearance to the group of disciples. True, Matthew connects this encounter with 'the other Mary'. But the author of the last chapter of Mark's Gospel and the evangelist John tell of a single astonishing encounter between Jesus and Mary Magdalene, which initiates her special role for all time.

As long as Mary Magdalene and the women still felt the physical nearness of Jesus, they were unshakeable in their faithfulness and perseverance. The one who died, the dead body, the corpse to be anointed and buried, connected them with him. Their cold dismay begins only when they come to the tomb on Easter morning and find that the body of Jesus is no longer there.

In my view, the encounter between Mary Magdalene and the risen Jesus can only be understood in the light of this special human and personal relationship with Jesus. John, with his predilection for extended conversations between Jesus and women, portrays the scene by the tomb which has been painted time and again: Mary Magdalene, all alone, in tears, hears a voice asking why she is weeping. Believing that it is the gardener, she complains that the body of her Lord has been taken away. Only when Jesus calls her by name, 'Mary', does she recognize him and cry out, 'My master'.

Up to that point everything is understandable, obvious and clear. But then comes the remark which is strange, cold, and rejecting, and which destroys all the feelings of returning happiness: 'Don't touch me! I have not yet returned to my Father.' Theologians have been bothered by it for centuries. They have toned it down, understood it in a positive way, have seen it as a logical contradiction to other encounters with the risen Jesus, where Thomas is invited to put his hand into the wound in Jesus' side or the women are invited to grasp his feet. In the prudish nineteenth century there were even references to the sexual dangers of such an encounter.

We cannot eliminate the shock which this remark necessarily causes. This is no longer the tender, friendly Jesus. It is no longer possible to touch or anoint his body. He cannot be brought back and held fast. Mary Magdalene may no longer spontaneously throw her arms around him.

The continuity which women seek is broken. The naiveté of childlike faith and trust is over. This is not the old Adam, of which masculine dogmatics always speaks in a way which seems so unconvincing to women. Rather, it is an instance of directness, totality, immediacy, spontaneity, an instance of childlike tenacity and perseverance, an instance of trust in this earth, in immortality and eternal duration.

Mary Magdalene experienced physical salvation in a way which went beyond almost everyone else. She loved Jesus personally. Without him, her life did not seem worth living. She showed tenacity and staying power. She never doubted him. But now she begins to cling to him. It is not the dead Messiah which makes her doubt, but the lost body of Jesus. It is here that she experiences death; here her existence falls apart.

I would prefer to translate the words 'Don't touch me' like this: 'Grow up, be mature! Accept the grief of parting.'

'Why do you seek the living among the dead?', the angel asks the women in the Gospel of Luke. It is the same message, and it means, 'Where you seek permanence there is only death. Where you are changed, there is life.' The 'sin' of women is not pride, but persistence.

Spontaneous childlike faith, however firm and permanent it may seem, must change and be submitted to the pain of parting. Only in this way can it grow up and mature.

The voice is still near and familiar, and in this voice Jesus is still the same. With this voice he gives her a task which does not do away with the distance now between them, but makes it comprehensible: his God is also the God of them all. His Father is also the Father of them all.

The apparently unbearable change becomes bearable. Mary Magdalene must go and speak of this new distance and nearness. Her pain and her terror go with her. Things are no longer as they were. But a task and a new community depend on her.

Up till now there has been little reflection on women's experiences of God. At the beginning of the experience of the disciples we find betrayal, and male theology is always constructed on the dialectic between betrayal and conversion. At the beginning of the experience of Mary Magdalene we find physical healing. She experienced wholeness. She was accepted into the Jesus community – body, mind and spirit. Because of that she does not run away, but remains. Because of that, she despairs when she can no longer feel this nearness. In her encounter with the risen Jesus she experiences the sorrow that the old order passes away, that nothing can be repeated, and that this is the only way in which new things can happen. The woman's conflict is between holding fast and letting go, between persevering and being open; this is a feminine dialectic which is not innate, but is rather inculcated, and which reflects social experiences.

Mary Magdalene may be regarded as the first apostle. She

The women of the Bible . . .

Mary Magdalene Proclaims the Resurrection to the Disciples.
Albani Psalter, Hildesheim, twelfth century.

. . . do not keep silent in church

Mary Magdalene Preaches in Aix.
Swiss school, beginning of the sixteenth century.

was the first to proclaim the gospel of the risen Jesus. This fact
was remembered down to the Middle Ages. But *her* message
was forgotten. Today, feminine experience and theology take
their place alongside patriarchal experience and theology. What
does she have to say to us, this woman who was healed, who
combines friendship and surrender, eros and agape? This
woman who to the last clings to this earth and relationships on
it, and who exhausts all hopes? This woman who learns that
resurrection means that she must not remain in this circle, but
learn to be open towards a new community? The theology of
Mary Magdalene has not yet been written. Perhaps the women
of today will succeed in writing it.

Biblical elements in the tradition about Mary Magdalene

How did the church cope with the offensive fact that Jesus had
a special love for a woman who was once mentally ill, and that
she became the first to proclaim the resurrection? As a patriarchal institution, how did it live with the fact that a woman
was instrumental in bringing it to birth? The answer to this
question can be found in the culture connected with Mary
Magdalene, which grew from the first stories about her in the
early church, through mediaeval legends, through the flourish-
ing art of the Middle Ages, down to the literature of modern
times. Here the story of Mary Magdalene was elaborated, and
formed the basis for further dreams, for dogmas and for moral
stances. Some areas of this culture have been constantly inves-
tigated and described. This is not the place to do even rough
justice to the various traditions or to make a survey of them.
I shall merely try to illuminate a number of traditions from
contemporary New Testament perspectives and the viewpoint
of a newly discovered image of women, and ask: which elements have been preserved, and have features of this Mary
Magdalene survived?

There has been constant reflection on three elements of her

story in the Bible: her call to proclaim the resurrection, her healing and her call, and her unusual relationship to Jesus.

(i) *Mary Magdalene preaching*

In the context of the contemporary Catholic debate about the ordination of women, Catholic feminist New Testament research – above all in the USA – has demonstrated that there was an apostolic women's ministry in the early church. One of its best known representatives was Mary Magdalene, who, according to many later witnesses, had a leading position in the early church. But just as today the Vatican reacts in an irritable and defensive way to this, so too the Pope's predecessor, Peter, was disturbed and offended that a woman should appropriate an apparently male role.

There is already a latent conflict within the New Testament: the women report the resurrection, but the disciples regard their story as mere gossip and speculation. They still have to have their own encounters with the risen Jesus. In the Gospel of John, Mary Magdalene reports only that the body of Jesus has been stolen. The disciples Peter and the one whom Jesus loved – in competition for apostleship – similarly had to have their own experiences. Here differences in status are seen even among the men: Peter runs faster, but the other one has greater faith. Paul knows of no appearances at all of the risen Jesus to women. However, hints in the Gospel of John that Jesus calls Mary Magdalene 'by name', that she thus belongs among 'his own' and is one of the sheep who hear his voice (John 10.3–5; 13.1; 20.16), even allow us to conclude that she was present at the Last Supper. Thus in John she is a bearer of the tradition in a concealed form, whereas the first three Gospels call only the Twelve disciples.

Her preferential position and the conflict between men and women is more obvious in those gospels which were composed later and were not taken into the New Testament. Peter above all appears as an offended, plaintive, zealous rival, who has tc take out his feelings on Jesus. 'My Lord,' he says in the *Pistis Sophia*, 'we cannot bear this woman any longer. She deprives us of any opportunity to say anything. She keeps on talking.'

'Would the Redeemer, then, have spoken secretly with a woman without letting us know? Should we perhaps repent and all listen to her?', he complains in the *Gospel according to Mary Magdalene*. At that point Mary Magdalene bursts into tears and asserts that she never invented her personal encounter with Jesus herself, and another disciple has to calm things down: Peter is not to treat the woman as an opponent. Doubtless Jesus knows her through and through, and has preferred her not only to all women, but also to all his friends.

According to the experiences of the early church, she is superior to men. She cheers up the helpless disciples, who do not know how they are to go about their task of preaching, in the same way that the angel cheers up the disciples in the Acts of the Apostles. Scenes of this kind can also be found in the painting of the eleventh and twelfth century: a crowd of ignorant disciples, at their wits' end, are on one occasion provided with a speech bubble: 'Tell us, Mary, what you saw on the way.' They are faced with a clearly superior Mary Magdalene who proclaims to them: 'I have seen the Lord.' Later the masculine monopoly of preaching was strengthened, and the scene increasingly vanished from art.

After her authority and spiritual sovereignty, the next most striking thing about Mary Magdalene is the visionary nature of her experience and her message. Now in antiquity the capacity to receive visions is in no way limited to women; however, in groups or institutions where patriarchal rational forms gained the upper hand, visionary and mystical modes of expression were quickly stamped out and marked as deviations. In so rational and also so masculine a century as the nineteenth, critics like David Friedrich Strauss mocked a Christianity which was based on the 'visions of a half-crazy woman'. Ernest Renan, author of a life of Jesus, noted gently, but disparagingly, the role of the 'clairvoyant' Mary Magdalene. The public from the first to the nineteenth century reacted with arrogance to the public activity of a woman. The message she presented to the world and the form in which she presented it was mocked as 'irrational'. Even in a later Gnostic writing Mary Magdalene had first to become a man in order to be saved. The church quickly lost the chance of becoming a community of men and women.

In the Middle Ages, there were occasional breaks in the tradition, which was increasingly accepted as being a male one. Granted, the documents of official mediaeval church history report hardly anything of this, but in the history of piety, which is still so often unnoticed, we can also find a positive evaluation of women. As we have noted in the Martha tradition, so too in southern France in the eleventh and twelfth centuries legends grew up around Mary Magdalene, as a result of which her role as the missionary saint to France became increasingly clear. According to the earliest legends she was exiled from Palestine and came to Provence with her spiritual director Maximinus. To begin with, the tradition about her is exclusively that of the great sinner, and for the reform movement of Cluny she became the symbol of the victory of spiritual over worldly life. Maximinus is still the real spiritual chief shepherd, who baptizes and preaches. However, a striking development then takes place: Mary Magdalene becomes emancipated from her spiritual director and in the second series of legends begins to preach, to convert, in one instance even to baptize. Lazarus and Martha, who are taken to be her kinsfolk, take their place alongside Maximinus and a certain bishop Cedonius. After this, however, it is noticeable that the spiritual masters retreat into the background and either become subordinate to the female figures, who are much more interesting, or are even made to look ridiculous, like the Lazarus who sleeps happily on Martha's lap in the Magdalene altar at Tiefenbronn. The women dominate and control the story. In the case of Martha, we already saw how in the story of the dragon an independent female counterpart to the male portrayal of George and the dragon comes into being. By comparison, Mary Magdalene, burdened with so many sensual 'feminine' traditions, found it much harder to attain independence. However, she does acquire a very active missionary role, converts the leading couple in Marseilles and their pagan subjects, and becomes the chief spiritual figure in the legends circulating in the south of France. Her specific function as an apostle, that of proclamation to the disciples, lives on in legend.

The rediscovery of Mary Magdalene the preacher can be seen in the stained-glass windows of French cathedrals of the thirteenth century. Here cycles of the legendary history of the saint are presented in which features of the New Testament Mary keep emerging, despite the alien mediaeval overtones. In Chartres cathedral, dating from 1230, Mary Magdalene is merely a saint with a halo – Martha still does not merit one – but her spiritual director Maximinus preaches the sermon. In Bourges cathedral, built fifteen years later, Martha too now has a halo. Women have increasing importance. In Auxerre cathedral, fifteen years later again, Mary Magdalene has progressed once more. She is preaching, and Maximinus is standing by. Her spiritual companion has clearly retreated into the shadows. However, the hierarchy is still preserved: Maximinus does the baptizing. At the end of the thirteenth century the two women, Mary Magdalene and Martha, are then depicted as preachers in the stained-glass windows of the cathedral at Sémur in Burgundy. Only in the sixteenth century at Chalons-sur-Marne do we find a picture in which Mary Magdalene, too, is baptizing. The woman has regained the role that she lost.

In the following period we also find portrayals of Mary Magdalene preaching in Florence, Lübeck, Donaueschingen and elsewhere. In Lübeck she can even be seen performing yet another function of the ministry: she is enthroning her brother Lazarus as bishop of Marseilles. In one manuscript illustration the Holy Spirit is hovering over her in the form of a dove. For a short period Mary Magdalene left her role as a sinner and returned to her task of proclamation. This brief, but impressive, emancipation ended with the Reformation.

What had happened? How could the taboo, the prohibition against a woman speaking in the community, have been broken so persistently in art?

In the case of Martha, we have already seen how the legends about her and the pictures to which they gave rise accorded with the feminist movement which came into being in the twelfth century in the south of France. Economic changes like the emergence of an industrial and commercial society, changes in laws of inheritance among the lesser country nobility which excluded daughters from inheriting to prevent a division of the estate, a surplus of women which was perhaps a result of the Crusades – all these were reasons why women looked for new openings and other ideals of life from those offered by the family. New spiritual and social forms of life arose over against the hierarchical church. Many groups demanded that possessions should be held in common and that each individual should have spiritual competence, and protests against the organized churches increased. Women in particular found new communities in groups like the Cathari and the Waldensians. Here one could find the woman who preached and discussed theology in public, and who corresponded to Mary Magdalene, the missionary.

Does the legend of Mary Magdalene and the art that goes with it come from such circles? Was it cherished among them above all else? At all events here, as in some of the early Christian Gnostic groups, we find a depreciation of Mary the mother of Jesus. Her place was taken by unconventional saints. In the Inquisition, to which many sectarian Christians and particularly women fell victim, reference was made, for example, to the perseverance of Mary Magdalene. However, we cannot prove that the cult of Mary Magdalene was fostered above all among the sects. Nevertheless, it is striking that the cult of Magdalene coincides in time with the feminist movement among the Cathari and the Waldensians and the altered image of the mature woman preacher, which torpedoes the church's tradition. Like Martha, Mary Magdalene too found her place in the hearts and minds of new charismatic revivals. No longer a sleeping beauty, her centuries-long charismatic personality awoke to new influence.

However, very early in the thirteenth century a retrograde hierarchical development began among the sects, which had once been so well disposed towards women. Furthermore, the bloody persecution of the Cathari brought the whole movement to an abortive end. Still, something of the twelfth-century revolution remained in the mediaeval women's movements of the following century. An authentic spiritualistic women's culture was preserved in the convents of the traditional orders which were springing up everywhere after the thirteenth century, and in the art of the subsequent period the independent spiritual figure of Mary Magdalene emerges every now and then. In reality her rights had now been curtailed: a male figure was again in charge of the nunnery. Until the twentieth century, public preaching by women again went underground.

(ii) The healing and call of a mentally ill woman

The church was even less able to cope with the second conflict, the demonic illness of a woman who had an intimate relationship with Jesus. Demonic possession of a woman? What was more natural to think of in this connection than unbridled lust, desire, extravagant sexuality? Even a Protestant commentator, Ernst Modersohn, who did not immediately brand her a sinner, used the example of the sick Mary Magdalene to warn against guilty and dominating passions. Mary Magdalene has become a monster, a prime example of sin and sexuality, because her exciting, choice and unique story was available for corresponding fantasies.

In sexual questions the early church remained profoundly uncertain, because of the practice of Jesus. The adulteress whom
Jesus did not condemn, the woman of Samaria whom he makes
the first apostle to the Samaritans, despite the blemishes in her
married life – all these were facts which it was difficult to cope
with in the solid development of Christian morality. Augustine
sighed over them and regretted that the story of the adulteress
was ever included in the Gospel of John. He explained the
earlier omission with 'reference to anxious husbands'.

Paul already differs from Jesus in providing more tangible
contrasts between the 'fleshly' and the 'spiritual'. Sin and
sexuality are brought into fatal proximity, even if they are not
identified. Immorality and idolatry are mentioned in the same
breath in Paul's catalogue of vices.

This was the starting point for later developments: demonic
illness was thought to arise from sexual obsessions, the apostle
became fused with the woman who was a sinner and Mary of
Bethany who anointed Jesus – and in this way came about the
greatest historical falsification in the West, in favour of patri-
archalism, which had the most influence on the place of women
in the church. The early Christian church fathers, e.g. Irenaeus,
Origen and Chrysostom, were still unfamiliar with the identification of the three women of the Bible. Was Augustine already
involved in it? According to Karl Künstle, he is already responsible for the confusion between the three women, 'which
was probably congenial to him for psychological reasons because it must have been a comfort for him that the Lord
resorted so often to Mary of Bethany, although she had once,
like him, been caught up in the toils of sensuality'. At all events,
Bishop Ambrose and other contemporaries and the moral
trend of the church seem to be responsible for creating a new
symbol for the relationship between body and spirit. This
development subsequently came to end with the homilies about
Magdalene given by Pope Gregory the Great about 600. Now
the ideal figure had been created who 'combined harmoniously

in one the penitence of the sinner, the zeal of Mary of Bethany and the love of Mary of Magdala' (Hans Hansel). Bolstered by the approval of the Pope, encouragement was now given to a picture of women which 'made a most vivid presentation of the help of divine grace and led to penitence which gave cause for hope' (Hans Hansel). The *magna peccatrix* Mary Magdalene was born, who stood representative for all the sins of the world and bore on her head a band which read, 'Do not doubt, you who have sinned! Through my example God renews you.'

Today we feel this to be a violation of an authentic image of women. Mary's artificially created portrait might have met moral needs, but her history could never again be read without falsification. Why did not Peter and his treachery become the example of sin and forgiveness? Why not Zacchaeus the publican with his corrupt dealings? Why were not the abandonment of a friend and social exploitation a better image of the corrupted person?

Western theology located sin one-sidedly and clearly in human corporeality, and specifically in woman. The lack of importance attached to them and the striking depreciation of their persons even today – in contrast to other cultures – was the result. The Greek theologians constantly maintained the distinction between the three women and thus found more varied, more attractive images of women. To identify the 'noble Mary of Bethany' with a harlot was contrary to their taste and their reverence for women.

Up until 1978 the German translation of the Roman Breviary cherished the image of *Maria poenitens* and the *magna peccatrix*. Then the falsification of the Bible was removed. However, the history of Western morality is still stamped by it. Magdalene convents, refuges and homes took pity on fallen girls. The attempts made since the end of the Middle Ages to disentangle the three women failed all too often. Luther did not follow the enlightened Faber Stapulensis, but popular feeling, and used Mary Magdalene as the ideal image of his doctrine of sin and grace. Granted, those Protestant theologians who were familiar with biblical criticism saw more clearly than their Catholic brothers how fatal the tradition was. However, that did not prevent the Home Mission in the last century from continuing to misuse the name of Magdalene. 'It is about time,' warned a theologian in 1903, 'that the home mission of the Protestant Church at least deleted the honourable name of Magdalene from its terminology and chose another more correct name for the prostitutes whom it welcomes.' Inquiries and present experience show that a long tradition of biblical criticism has hardly been successful in connecting other ideas than that of the great sinner with the name of Mary Magdalene. What is needed to overcome this sexism?

Mary Magdalene would need to encounter us anew as a completely healed person. However, we are still suffering from a theology which separates body, soul and spirit and has not made it possible for us to rediscover our body as God's good creation. Mary Magdalene was the image of the way in which people dealt with their bodies and their spirits: condemnation of sensuality and glorification of that which goes beyond the senses, the subjection of the earth and the triumph of the spirit over the earthbound. As Hans Hansel says, by means of her image, 'the early Christian sought . . . to free the soul from its connection to the body in order to make it easier for it to ascend into the purely spiritual realm of the divine'. Her image was a great attraction to those who visited Vézelay, in southern France, the place of pilgrimage consecrated to her, before embarking on the Crusades. It was here that Bernard of Clairvaux preached the victory of the Christian cross over pagan unbelief. The world-denying spirit of the Cluniac reform made use of her, and the Franciscan mendicant orders wanted to reform the church with the aid of her conquest of the world.

The picture which finally established itself as the church's picture, composed of the various representations of Magdalene, shows her 'elevation'. She hovers gently above the earth. A cherub lifts up one of her feet and another cherub raises the other foot from the ground. The sinner is victor over the world. This picture has wrongly tended to be interpreted as the ascension of Mary Magdalene. In fact it represents her heavenly elevation while at prayer, a scene which derives from the group of southern French legends mentioned above. From the late Middle Ages down to the Baroque period, even in the time of the Reformation, when Dürer made many copies from his woodcut of the 'elevation' which were sold in the markets, this picture of woman became predominant and now brought the active tradition about Mary Magdalene to an abortive end. 'She had fallen victim to the over-sensuous world . . .' we now read in a Catholic interpretation of the saints. She had now succeeded in rising from the dangers of sensuality into pure spheres. However, her corporeality had been suppressed.

(iii) *The friend of Jesus*

From earliest times the Johannine Easter encounter between Jesus and Mary Magdalene has provoked conjectures about a particularly intimate relationship between the two of them. In their brief dialogue, in his call 'Mary', in her reply 'My Master', there seem to be a delight, a happiness, an eroticism which transcend the teacher-pupil relationship.

Mary Magdalene had fulfilled a basic human need for eroticism which was not satisfied by the New Testament. One man countered my remarks about Mary Magdalene, the first woman apostle, with the anxious question as to where, in that case, any eroticism was left. The apostolate of women destroyed the original erotic image of Mary Magdalene for him. Thus in Christianity, with its anxieties about sex, she has also had to take up and satisfy erotic needs. Perhaps that was her most open, cheerful and sympathetic function.

It was as a result of this that, first of all, she became the patron saint of the cosmetic industry in the Middle Ages. Makers of perfume, blenders of **unguents and coiffeurs** all put

Mary Magdalene, sensuously beautiful, is elevated by
the angels at prayer

Mary Magdalene. The Elevation.
Pilgrimage Church of Madonna d'Ongero in Carona,
near Lugano. First half of the eighteenth century.

themselves under her protection. Fashionable accessories like handbags, combs and gloves all formed part of the fascination of women. She also presided over their manufacture. Painters portrayed her in elegant flowing robes adorned with jewellery. In some sixteenth- and seventeenth-century paintings she admired, half-naked, her own beauty. Alongside the suppressed threat that this is vanity, empty vanity, one can detect the pleasure, the delight of prudish Christianity in depicting the sensuous side of life. The fair Helen of Christianity also prances beside her lover, rides to the hunt and, emancipated from the church, becomes the embodiment of sheer sensual delight.

The standard works about women in the New Testament have tended to make us forget this. The Catholic Ketter sees her rather as the leader of a Catholic group of women devoted to their bishop, and the Protestant Leipoldt sees her as a modest and restrained Protestant woman endowed with emotional virtues.

Jesus, too, was so much the subject of dogma, and therefore so removed from the sphere of sex, that for a long time his private relationships were taboo. However, contemporary questions about people in their social relationships have also put the personal life of the rabbi Jesus in a new light. It is inconceivable, thinks Shalom Ben Chorim, that a rabbi should not have been married. However, this matter-of-fact-course is not mentioned at all in the New Testament. In his modern biography of Jesus, Jean Claude Barreau solves the problem by making Jesus a widower. After a short marriage, his wife Sarah died. By means of this device he removes Jesus from any conflicts of sexual ethics and makes him a model example of the relationship between men and women. The humanity of Jesus has been preserved.

Particularly in recent years there has been a passionate discussion of the question whether Jesus had intimate relationships with Mary Magdalene. The imaginary unrest which John

THE WOMEN AROUND JESUS

has created here has indeed undergone spiritual sublimation: Mary Magdalene, the bride of Christ, betrothed but not married, a marriage which is promised but not consummated, a spiritual bride and a spiritual bridegroom. But Luther had strong words to say about her earthly love for Jesus: 'All she can think, dream and say is, if only I had this husband, my dearest guest and master, my heart would be content.' She loved him 'warmly and passionately,' she had a 'hot and burning heart' towards him. These expressions have suggested that Luther assumed that there were sexual relationships between the two. But then he interprets their 'daily communion' to mean that they were brought together into a 'familiarity', not just in an earthly fashion, but also in spiritual terms. The word *familiaritas* which he uses here is subsequently translated as 'brotherhood', so that we are to assume that he imagined that there was an inner friendship between the two. Perhaps this did not exclude sexual relationships, because she set on him 'goodness and honour, body and life, and all that she had'. However, he wanted to show her above all as the embodiment of the completely spontaneous and passionate surrender of faith.

The 'great lover' has increasingly taken an independent form in modern times. The relationship with Jesus has become looser. She made history, above all in France, as the courtesan who loved much and therefore was forgiven much. In German literature in the last century the Nobel Prizewinner Paul Heyse made her an Epicurean who sees fulfilment in sensuality: 'She embodies pleasure, the free will in us simply to still the hunger of our senses, to enjoy all the delights of youth and not to ask whether we shall perhaps hate tomorrow what we have loved today . . .'

Instead of being a sensuously erotic makeweight in Christianity, Mary Magdalene is now being rediscovered in theology as a lover.

Ernst Eggimann writes,

MARY MAGDALENE

> I imagine this night
> outside history
> which transcended all morality.

Eros and agape, sensual love and caritative surrender, which had long been separated, at least in Protestantism, now find each other.

> When you put your arm around her
> her surrender was
> as great
> as a divine love.

Something which cannot be provided by any other feminine figure, and was not disclosed even by the motherly love of Mary, emerges again with Heinrich Böll's demand for Mary Magdalene's tenderness: a Christianity which is well disposed to sexuality, which meets men and their needs, and whose moral laws should be re-examined. We certainly do not do Mary Magdalene justice if we associate her only with great love and surrender. When we connect her closely with tenderness, she is misused as compensation for a rough world. When we want erotic needs to be satisfied by her, she becomes one-dimensional. Mary Magdalene as the addition of tenderness to a gruesome crucifixion story and to a harsh patriarchal world completely by-passes the total view of the New Testament and its women.

This helpless therapy of the world by women is dramatized in the rock opera *Jesus Christ Superstar*: Mary Magdalene and the group of women are to the suffering and lonely Jesus what no man can be to him. 'She alone has tried to give me what I need right here and now,' the author makes Jesus say, and, 'There is not a man among you who knows or cares if I come or go.' The women surround Jesus like nurses, and while Mary Magdalene speaks hypnotically to him, to make him relax, to close his eyes, to think of nothing and to let the world be the world, the others mutter in confirmation, as though in a refrain,

'Ev'rythings alright yes ev'rythings alright yes ev'rythings alright.'

Mary Magdalene is more than the feminine confidential partner of Jesus. Her erotic traits still make their mark on us today. This is part of her personality, of what makes her a complete person. But her eroticism may be freed from the ghetto of a sexuality understood in narrow terms, and flow over into different relationships.

One of the rare pictures of the anointing of Jesus' head

The Anointing.
Illustration, 1260, in the Psalter of a Cistercian Convent in Basel.
Municipal Library, Besançon.

4

THE UNKNOWN WOMAN
WHO ANOINTED JESUS

Jesus was in Bethany at the house of Simon, a man who had suffered from a dreaded skin disease. While Jesus was eating, a woman came in with an alabaster jar full of a very expensive perfume made of pure nard. She broke the jar and poured the perfume on Jesus' head. Some of the people there became angry and said to one another, 'What was the use of wasting the perfume? It could have been sold for more than three hundred silver pieces and the money given to the poor!' And they criticized her harshly. But Jesus said 'Leave her alone! Why are you bothering her? She has done a fine and beautiful thing for me. You will always have poor people with you, and any time you want to, you can help them. But you will not always have me. She did what she could; she poured perfume on my body to prepare it ahead of time for burial. Now, I assure you that wherever the gospel is preached all over the world, what she has done will be told in memory of her' (Mark 14.3–9).

For Mark this woman is the first to recognize the central importance of the passion of Jesus. Here 'faith in the gospel' is fulfilled in a unique way. So in Mark she stands at the beginning of the passion and by her action stresses that Jesus' way to death (and perhaps there is also already an explicit thought of the resurrection) is the decisive heart of the message (Eduard Schweizer).

The king of all kings is anointed, and now he is crowned king
at the very point that he goes to suffering. Suffering is the way
to kingly rule. That had already been proclaimed in all the
announcements of the passion ... But of all the disciples of
Jesus, only a woman understands this ... Still, elsewhere too
in the Gospels it is women who believe for others, and remain
faithful for others; and at that time women, like children and
the uneducated, were among the despised who were denied a
full share in the kingdom of heaven. A fundamentally different
situation is created here only through Jesus and in his community. But in this way the woman is the first to proclaim
'this' gospel of the good news of Jesus' death and resurrection
(Julius Schniewind).

In the New Testament there is a theology of what I would dare
to call tenderness, which always has a healing effect: through
words, through the laying on of hands, which one can also call
caressing, through kisses, a meal together – in my view all this
is totally destroyed and distorted by legalization, one might
well say by the Roman approach which has made this into
dogmas, principles and catechisms; this element in the New
Testament, that of tenderness, has certainly not yet been discovered (Heinrich Böll).

An unknown story

The unknown woman who makes her way into a closed male
gathering, breaks a flask of precious ointment, pours its con-
tents over Jesus' head and then disappears back into the darkness of history is one of the most generous and most obscure
feminine figures in the New Testament.

Unknown? Are we not all familiar enough with the story of
the anointing and the pictorial representations of it? The alabaster flask, the woman among a circle of men, the saying of
Jesus that her action would never be forgotten?

94

THE UNKNOWN WOMAN WHO ANOINTED JESUS

What we usually know of is the anointing of Jesus' feet by a woman. And this woman is regarded as a great sinner, or as Mary Magdalene.

The present story begins in a different way and *is* a different one; it appears in the oldest Gospel, and is probably the oldest tradition about the anointing of Jesus by a woman; it tells of an unknown figure who anoints Jesus' head, and tempts us to read the anointing of Jesus for once in terms of *this* woman and *this* anointing.

First of all we must remember the time and place of this remarkable action: it is two days before the Jewish feast of the Passover. Jesus has come to Jerusalem with his group. His arrest is imminent. The Jewish authorities have resolved to strike and to do away with this radical, offensive revolutionary, who attracts such a large following. The men who have accompanied him from the early days have become increasingly confused and doubtful. They fundamentally misunderstand him. They cannot bring themselves to imagine that this hopeless revolution might end with suffering and death. They protest when Jesus speaks of his death (8.32); anxiety seizes them (10.32). And to crown these growing misunderstandings, at the beginning of the final journey to Jerusalem we have the foolish request of the two disciples who want Jesus to give them prominent places of honour (10.35ff.).

Not only is Jesus threatened with arrest; he also becomes an isolated figure. More than any other evangelist, Mark, the author of the earliest Gospel, depicts Jesus as human, lonely, torn apart, prey to his body and his anxieties. In Gethsemane Jesus 'trembles'. His hope that the bitter end will pass by him is a real one, and is not blurred by any expression of obedience added at a later date. In Mark, Jesus does not die, either, in harmony with the will of God, but with an inarticulate cry, full of intrinsic discord, at odds with himself, his body, his fate and his God.

Shortly before the catastrophe, the unknown woman pours

95

over Jesus, forsaken and in process of being torn apart, a sense-less amount of the most precious perfumed Indian oil. To anoint a guest was really something that a courteous host should have done. Here the host had failed, and the woman took over his role. However, this eccentric squandering of so much oil, representing the annual wages of a labourer, must have seemed crazy and arrogant. Oils were regarded as a luxury, imported from the East. In the Roman Empire they were used to an extent which provoked moral displeasure. They were often regarded as 'unmanly', as a sign of femininity, and were condemned by 'real men'. The company at the dinner party depicted in Mark's Gospel also consisted of real men, who voted for social utility and against decadence: 'Think what one could have done for the poor with the proceeds!'

Two questions arise.

First, who is the woman? Was she one of that group of Galilean women who accompanied Jesus right from the begin-ning of his activity in Galilee, or was she by herself?

Secondly, what does such an anointing mean? What was its original significance?

Let us consider the second question first. If we are to under-stand again what the original anointing meant, we must remove various layers of débris from our understanding and forget the patriarchal way in which we have been conditioned to interpret the story. We regard 'anointing' as a strictly feminine practice. A group of women who occupied themselves with New Testa-ment texts about women in order to discover more about them-selves came to grief on the passage about the women who wanted to anoint the dead body of Jesus on Easter morning: 'Again, isn't that typically feminine? What would it mean for women today?'

In fact, in the middle-class Western world, anointing has always been connected with cosmetics, with the care of the sick and with loving actions, and has been commended to women as their very own sphere. Fliedner saw the women who went to anoint Jesus as models for his nursing sisters. Like going to the cemetery or lamenting the dead, anointing by 'the tender hands of women', in Shalom Ben Chorim's phrase, is now regarded in our culture as a specifically feminine role. The flask of oil has become the symbol of almost all female saints.

Furthermore, Mary of Bethany, Mary Magdalene and the woman who was a great sinner have been rolled into one, sin and anointing have been connected together, and anointing has been understood as a woman's way of making good.

But who would anoint in ancient times?

A host would anoint his guests to refresh them. Dead bodies were anointed, to preserve them, and as a mark of reverence. Sick people were anointed as a cure. Mark records that the disciples did this. And kings were anointed. Anointing was not a task restricted to women. For example, no woman ever anointed an Israelite king!

Once we have done away with these two common errors, namely, that we are dealing with a woman with a past and an action carried out only by the tender hands of a woman, we have come one step nearer to our unknown figure.

Who is she? And what sort of a woman is she?

She is bold and unashamed, tender and compassionate; presumably a solitary figure, more radical than the group of women around Jesus, but close to them. It does not trouble her to break with tradition and any sense of propriety. She goes against accepted manners to do something good for Jesus. She anoints him in the same way as one anoints a dead body, and in so doing shows up the disciples, who are in love with success and who still cannot see that the way of Jesus will lead to death. She does not want to delay him on this way, but simply to take her place beside him. She is not confused and anxious, but full of sympathy, full of com-passion.

And she also breaks with ancient Israelite traditions: she assumes a male role. In ancient Israel, they anointed the one who had been chosen as the new king. At God's bidding, the prophet Samuel anointed Saul (and later David) as king, pouring a flask of oil on his head. That is what the unknown woman now does to Jesus. However, she is not a famous prophet but an unknown woman, and Jesus does not expect any historical task, but a shameful death. John and Luke describe how his feet are anointed; Mark – and, following him, Matthew – describes the anointing of his head. Both increasingly allude to Israelite traditions. Thus the unknown woman is at the same time a prophet who anoints the Messiah, consecrates him and equips him for his task. This is a twofold break with the patriarchal tradition: the king is a candidate for death and Israel is under foreign rule, and an anonymous woman takes on the role of the 'men of Judah' (II Sam. 2.4). Here is the proclamation of a new age in which old values will be turned upside down.

Priestess, witch, or wise woman?

This great unknown woman displays, beyond doubt, features of the wise woman familiar from all religions, who heals and who prophesies the future. Granted, these features do not match parallels in the history of religions: the sibyls, fairies and witches with their healing unguents. However, something of their magic emerges here. The vessel containing oil, the alabaster flask, recalls the magical jug or pot which is always to be found 'in the hand of the feminine mana figure, the priestess or later the witch' (Erich Neumann).

Such women appear rarely in biblical history, and where they do, they are very much in the background. The age-old stubborn fight against mother goddesses, the female forces of healing, primal matriarchal forms, which began in Israel and continued in Christianity, has also hardened our views about the relics of such primal pictures. But the unknown woman emerges like a wise woman, knows the future more fully and more clearly than anyone else, without bearing the fatal traits of a cheerless goddess of destiny. She comforts Jesus and anoints him with healing ointment. And in addition she takes over a political role: she chooses the king.

Mereschkowski has set the unknown woman alongside the great unknown Jesus, who similarly escapes us whenever we want to hold him fast: 'the unknown woman stands beside the unknown man, the bride beside the bridegroom'. He has made this woman see in Jesus' death the new beginning, 'the birth pangs of the whole of mother earth, who is to bring forth the kingdom of God'. The theologians of the Eastern church also discover in her the matriarchal images which have been forgotten in Christianity.

Eduard Schweizer hints at the possibility of a vision of the resurrection: 'Perhaps there is also already an explicit notion of the resurrection.' The women who, in the Gospel of Mark, go to the tomb on Easter morning also carry ointments. What is this meant to suggest?

According to Mark, the disciples have the task of healing and driving out evil spirits. And we are explicitly told that they anoint and heal the sick (6.13). Did the women at the tomb and the unknown woman want to perform this messianic healing on the body of Jesus? Were they already hinting at the body of the risen Jesus?

People quickly ruled out this uncanny phenomenon and gave the anonymous woman a name and a history. However, the commentators who deal with this Marcan story today still continue to lose some of their masculine self-confidence, and the unknown woman continues to shake the patriarchal dominance of theology: a woman knew of the messianic secret before all the disciples.

The unknown woman can look back on a varied history. Anything numinous, magical, prophetic, perhaps even pagan, was terrifying. People wanted to be able to get hold of such mysterious phenomena and draw them into the understandable everyday world. Theologians soon got their hands on them, 'liberated' them from anonymity and gave them a name and a history. For Luke this astonishing action, which put the disciples in the shade, was the act of a great sinner who anointed Jesus' feet. A prostitute known throughout the town, a woman who was in everyone's bad books, performed the unusual, provocative and costly loving service. The act was made into a private and personal one. The earlier history of the woman provides the reason for her eccentric action. Despite the historical significance of the anointing as a reference to Jesus' death, Luke is interested here in the guilt and redemption of a woman to whom he gives a personal history, if not a name.

John associated the same action with the sensitive Mary of Bethany. From the time of Augustine on, the act was laid on the shoulders of Mary Magdalene, made into the great sinner, as an act of expiation for a wasted life. Subsequently, anointing and expiation provided artists of all ages with a favourite theme, a summons to repentance and conversion. The anointing then went on to have a significance of its own as a great act of love, without any reference to Jesus at all. This gave rise to the literary figure of the woman 'who loved much and therefore was forgiven much'. The great unknown woman had been brought under control: one could grasp her and understand her. And she was changed into the typical feminine deterrent of a seduced and seductive woman. We can only guess at the extent to which these elaborations of the tradition have led to discrimination against women of all times. The hidden history of the women around Jesus to be found in Mark is rarely disclosed, and even now it has escaped the awareness of a number of theologians.

The noble figure of the woman who anointed the Messiah barely appears in the world of art. Would it not have been possible to hint at the lordship of Jesus in such a picture? The lordship of a woman over a man? A relationship of superior to inferior which might have been capable of misunderstanding? Whereas the anointing of Jesus' feet became a favourite theme of painters, we rarely find pictures of the anointing of Jesus' head. Round about 1260, a picture of the Last Supper was painted for the Psalter of a Cistercian convent, in which a woman in nun's dress is standing behind Jesus and pouring oil over his head. Was this commissioned, or even painted by the nuns, who at this time were arriving at a sense of independence and self-awareness? Did they make concessions to the tradition by representing a woman under the table, anointing the feet of Jesus? In body language, a woman towering head and shoulders above Jesus, and performing a masculine, prophetic action on him, did not quite correspond with the Christian ideal of women. The humble, servile attitude of anointing the feet had suppressed an ancient, early Christian recollection.

It is impossible to provide a complete solution to the riddle of this remarkable figure of a woman to be found in the early church. Perhaps it is enough for us to rediscover, in our own day, those traits which have been forgotten: her act of eman cipation and her function in a Christianity which ignores the body, is dominated by men, and is all too prone to rationality and verbosity: the physical solidarity and the healing community which a woman announces as the new messianic order.

Corporeality in Mark

People have bodies and feelings; they feel well, they hurt, they feel lonely, they sense delight. For Mark, the gospel can be felt and sensed, and he had an unparalleled way of expressing the corporeality of the experience of joy, well-being and sorrow. For us in a Western Christianity, where the body is forgotten or suppressed, or is a vehicle for achieving one's ends, many passages in his Gospel sound remarkably archaic. In our ver bose and literate church, dumb actions always need a word of explanation. We fill the silence with words or music. Matthew and Luke, who preach and give verbal interpretations a great deal, are much closer to us.

101

In Mark, the disciples are sent out to demonstrate the time of salvation by saving actions, anointing the sick and driving out demons. The healings performed by Jesus are physical, primal and described in detail. He mixes spittle and earth and applies them to the eyes of a blind man (8.23). He puts his fingers in the ears of a deaf man and touches his tongue (7.33).

Whereas in Matthew, some detachment is already preserved or the physical aspect is minimized, in Mark there is still touching, and physical proximity. Jesus first of all makes Peter's mother-in-law sit up in bed before he gives her his hand and heals her (1.31). First of all he embraces the children tenderly and caresses them before using them as an illustration for his teaching (9.36; 10.16). The first thing he does after raising Jairus' daughter is to have her given something to eat.

In Mark, Jesus himself is more of a human being, more physical than in the other Gospels. He enjoys the gesture of anointing. He trembles with anguish in Gethsemane. He dies with an inarticulate cry, and the whole attitude of obedience which was added later has still not destroyed the image of the feeling, suffering man who looks for human proximity. He is also more sensitive towards examples of wretchedness. He is often 'grieved'. He has a 'heart'. He surrenders himself in his whole person.

This Jesus needs people. He is not the solitary hero. He is not so sovereign that he can do without his neighbour. The betrayal by the disciples grieves him, and in Gethsemane this grief makes him tremble physically. The luxurious anointing comes from the comforting proximity of women: delight, enjoyment, pleasure, in a solitude that is becoming increasingly painful. If we did not have the Gospel of Mark, we would have a much cooler, more 'divine' picture of Jesus. Mark has brought us the gentle Jesus.

However, the physical nature of this Jesus, which he brings with him, this openness for himself, his sorrow, his joy, his nearness to others, also provokes conflicts with those around.

THE UNKNOWN WOMAN WHO ANOINTED JESUS

Every culture has its phobias about touch. These appear above all in taboos about sexuality and their social effects. In ancient society the human body was taboo, i.e. untouchable, when it was unclean, leprous or dead. Anyone who touched such a body transgressed ritual laws and themselves became unclean, i.e. they could not participate in any religious cults.

In a sovereign way, Jesus puts himself above these taboos. For him they do not exist. He touches the lepers and heals them. He allows himself to be touched by them, and they become healthy. What we find miraculous plays a central role in the gospel: the breakthrough to a body of our own which is regarded as entirely God's good creation, which is not isolated by any illness and which no ritual laws can despise and present as untouchable.

In the same way, Jesus breaks through the taboo surrounding a dead body: he touches the dead daughter of Jairus. The other two raisings of dead persons in the New Testament, Lazarus and the young man from Nain, reported by John and Luke respectively, do not involve any touch. Did Mark simply make Jesus break the taboo in a provocative way? And did he deliberately demonstrate this by means of the dead girl?

The third taboo, contact with an unclean, i.e. menstruating woman, happens in the story of the woman with an issue of blood (Mark 5.24ff.). In 'a shocking way', according to Eduard Schweizer, Mark tells how the liberation of human beings extends even into unmentionable areas of the body. When Jesus is being summoned to Jairus' house, a woman in the crowd comes up to him from behind and touches his robe. For twelve years she had had chronic haemorrhages; she had been wealthy, but in the meantime she had spent her money on doctors who had been quite unable to help her. Impoverished, delivered over to her sick body and to social death, there was no hope for her. When, as a last resort, she touched Jesus' garment, the haemorrhage stopped. The story is also told by Matthew and Luke. However, only Mark stresses that 'She felt in her body that she had been made whole' (5.9). Here the gospel has become tangible. Here liberation has been experienced physically. Here something has been made new, even down to a person's physical and spiritual marrow.

Now, however, Jesus also 'feels' something: a power has gone out of him. Furthermore, he has become ritually unclean. The woman has involved him in her fate. She becomes clean, and he becomes unclean.

Perhaps it is no coincidence that this episode has become embedded in the story of the raising of Jairus' daughter: Jesus becomes unclean not only through a dead woman but also through a menstruating one. He does away with these laws; he shows them to be of no effect, by giving both women new life.

An old manuscript contains the accusation that Jesus led women and children astray into impurity. This did not appear in the official accusation before Pilate. Is that also a taboo? The practice of the later church again cultivated these laws of purity. Down to our own day there are areas in the church in which women have no prospects because they are suspected of being impure.

Corporeality is no sphere reserved for women. In Mark, men too experience a healing change in their bodies. However, particular women experienced physical liberation more directly than men. Therefore, also in Mark, there emanates from them a wordless, healing, comforting power which embraces the whole person. On Easter morning they risk the same great transgression of a taboo as their master: they want to anoint a dead body and in an undisturbed way continue the physical proximity which they have experienced. However, the dead body is no longer there. The physical experience is not the only one, nor the last one. It is threatened by the death and destruction of the body, but despite this it is essential, because it bears within it the hope for the new heaven and the new earth.

'When you love, you aren't afraid . . .'

The Gospel of the Peasants of Solentiname.
Jugenddienstverlag Wuppertal.

5

THE GROUP OF WOMEN
IN MARK

So they arrested Jesus and held him tight . . . Then all the
disciples left him and ran away.

The army officer who was standing there in front of the cross
saw how Jesus had died. 'This man was really the Son of God,'
he said. Some women were there, looking on from a distance.
Among them were Mary Magdalene, Mary the mother of the
younger James and of Joseph, and Salome. They had followed
Jesus while he was in Galilee and had helped him. Many other
women who had come to Jerusalem with him were there
also . . .

Joseph bought a linen sheet, took the body down, wrapped
it in the sheet and placed it in a tomb which had been dug out
of solid rock. Then he rolled a large stone across the entrance
to the tomb. Mary Magdalene and Mary the mother of Joseph
were watching and saw where the body of Jesus was placed.
After the Sabbath was over, Mary Magdalene, Mary the
mother of James, and Salome bought spices to go and anoint
the body of Jesus. Very early on Sunday morning at sunrise,
they went to the tomb . . .

They entered the tomb, where they saw a young man sitting
on the right, wearing a white robe – and they were alarmed.
'Don't be alarmed,' he said, 'I know you are looking for Jesus
of Nazareth, who was crucified. He is not here – he has been
raised: Look, here is the place where they put him. Now go

and give this message to his disciples, including Peter: "He is going to Galilee ahead of you; there you will see him, just as he told you." ' So they went out and ran from the tomb, distressed and terrified. They said nothing to anyone, because they were afraid (Mark 14.46, 50; 15.39, 40, 41, 46, 47; 16.1f·, 5–8).

None of his disciples saw how Jesus died (Mereschkowski).

The disciples of Jesus had their doctrine crossed out in a way which so threw them off course that they could only flee (Eduard Schweizer).

In Mark's theological perspective women are the functional successors of Jesus and they represent the true intention of Jesus and his mission within the messianic people of God (Elisabeth Schüssler-Fiorenza).

So to our surprise Mark lifts the curtain on a quite unknown part of the life of Jesus, the Unknown, in which the feminine rather than the masculine prevails. The purely masculine gospel extends as far as Golgotha, and after that we have the feminine one . . .
    All the disciples had fled, had 'denied' him; only the women who followed him remained true to him. The weak women were stronger than the men: the faith of Peter the rock ran away like sand; the faith of Mary, however, was truly a rock. The love of men proved powerless; the love of women was strong. The sun of man's love set in death, but the sun of woman's love arises in the resurrection (Mereschkowski).

It was women who went first to the tomb and not men; women are braver than men (A peasant woman from Solentiname in Nicaragua).

108

THE GROUP OF WOMEN IN MARK

A subversive story

The peasant women of Nicaragua whom I mentioned at the beginning of this book are right: in the gospel, women have more courage and heart. Women have a special role: in the Gospel of Mark there is a story about women which puts the story of the disciples in the shade.

Outwardly, it all seems like a man's story, and the women's story is hidden. Jesus calls twelve disciples. They follow him from Galilee, are sent out for a work of mission and healing, take part in the Last Supper and are in constant conversation with Jesus until, when he is arrested, they flee.

The story of the women takes a subversive course, underground. It tells how women from Galilee accompanied Jesus right from the start, had the closest personal contact with him, served him as he served them. At least one woman foresaw his death. None of them were frightened by his arrest. All remained in close proximity to Jesus as he was condemned and executed. Even after his death they were full of his person and his message. They were there at the burial of Jesus, and an indeterminate hope drove them to the tomb on Easter morning. The empty tomb terrified them profoundly, made them helpless and lonely. The news of Jesus' resurrection given by the young man threw them completely off course, so that they fled and were beside themselves. Did they suspect that what Jesus said had been fulfilled? They could not hand on the terrifying secret, although the young man at the tomb had told them to.

That brings the Gospel of Mark proper to an end. A conclusion appended later (16.9ff.) tells of further Easter encounters of Jesus with women and men.

The basic idea running through this Gospel of Mark is that God reveals himself in human suffering and that this can be experienced in following Jesus, sharing in his life and suffering. However, the male, human story is a story of complete failure:

109

the Pharisees, the citizens of Nazareth, and finally the disciples fail. The story of the disciples is the most tragic. Jesus called them to personal discipleship and for a while – for example, in Peter's confession – they followed him. However, in the central portion of the Gospel the three great misunderstandings arise: Jesus tells them that his life will end, not with success, but with failure. This confuses, dismays and disappoints the group, which reacts first with resistance, then with dumb desperation and finally with paralysis (Mark 8.32; 9.30f.; 10.32). From time to time they still have naive dreams of sharing in power and glory. Thus the brothers John and James (10.35) want to sit at his right hand, i.e. to have legitimate participation in his rule. But in the last part, on the way of the passion, towards Jerusalem, the final failure takes place: Judas betrays Jesus. The others flee when he is arrested.

As far as human capabilities are concerned, the Gospel of Mark seems to be a hopeless book. 'That his disciples fail again and again shows once more how impossible the knowledge of God is for man.' So writes Eduard Schweizer. For 'only the disciple will be able to understand the power of the words and actions of Jesus'.

But who are his disciples?

Schweizer sees hope first and foremost for the Gentiles, for whom Mark expects this knowledge and this discipleship even more. For the disciples who fail there remains the prospect of being able to 'follow' the Risen Lord. This message is to be passed on by the women, who have a greater staying power. But this shows Mark's perspective, which has hitherto been concealed and which is not usually noticed at all: where the disciples fail, the women are the true disciples. Where men 'have their dogmatics crossed out', women begin to live. Where official history ends in darkness, the underground has a history of its own. What does it look like? And where does the underground come to the surface?

The group of women does not just accompany Jesus from

110

Galilee; it also does what it has come for: it serves (15.41). In this way the women fulfil Jesus' instruction, 'He who would be great among you, let him be your servant,' and follow the one who has come 'to serve and to give his life a ransom for many' (9.35; 10.42ff.). As I have shown earlier, they stay with him in suffering, death and burial. They stand 'far off', not out of anxiety, but because the place of execution was cordoned off by the military. There is also a report of two women who were present at the burial of Jesus by the councillor Joseph of Arimathea (15.47). According to Mark, three women were witnesses of what happened at Easter and are said to have been the first heralds of the resurrection (16.1ff.). Finally it is a woman – the unknown woman – who in contrast to the disciples, rivalling one another for success, understands the death of Jesus and puts herself at his side (14.3–9). The small group of weeping, but brave women, who in any case have nothing to lose – as has been a widespread view right down to today – takes on profile and stands out from the larger group of women disciples proper.

Time and again, in other Gospels as well, women are said to have 'served' – to have been true disciples of Jesus. Peter's mother-in-law serves, Martha serves, the group of Galilean women serve. This discipleship is never reported of the disciples. Thus in all the Gospels there is still a remnant of ancient experience that women were the real followers, wage-earners and participants in the life of Jesus. In Mark, 'to serve' is not a humiliating activity but a mutual giving and taking, a self-surrender and mutual acceptance, an exchange of love, tenderness, help and comfort. In that case Jesus did not just have women as disciples; for some circles in the early church they were the *real* disciples.

After all this, it must be assumed that in the communities which Mark knew, women were regarded as exemplary disciples and therefore also occupied leading positions.

Mereschkowski has already referred to this unknown Mark,

and the American scholar Elisabeth Schüssler has now demonstrated convincingly 'that in Mark's theological perspective women are the functional successors of Jesus and they represent the true intention of Jesus and his mission within the messianic people of God'.

Today theological scholarship is agreed that the women were the real transmitters of the tradition of the death, burial and resurrection of Jesus. Who but the women could have told of the events on Golgotha?

However, scholars also believe that there was a much richer and more varied tradition about women than is suggested by the stories about women and the concealed tradition of the group of women. According to Elisabeth Schüssler, we still see only 'the tip of an iceberg'. According to Hartwig Thyen, 'as these groups were lost in history, so too the greatest part of their testimony disappeared. The documents of the church's fight against heresy suggest that in this testimony the liberation of woman from man's domination, as furthered by Christ, had its own role . . .'

In a patriarchal society which began to shape the early communities at a very early stage, the shameful role played by the disciples according to the early tradition could not last for long. The other Gospels disguise the defect and restore honour to the men.

The Gospel of Mark, the oldest source we have, still tells us clearly that all the disciples of Jesus fled and that women were present at the execution (15.40f.). In parallel to this, Matthew describes the flight of the disciples and similarly mentions, three times, the group of women at Jesus' execution, burial and resurrection. Only individual women's names vary.

Only in Luke do we find the church's view, which is still common even today: the flight of the disciples is not mentioned. Alongside the women under the cross there are also many acquaintances, who are even named for the first time, and perhaps in this way Luke is indicating the preponderance of men.

The special role of the women, still known to the early tradition, is concentrated on their presence at the tomb and on Easter morning. Luke, who also restricted the role of the women in other cases, created the picture of a church where parity prevailed.

John, who was not interested in any historical tradition, presented two stylized figures, the beloved disciple and his mother, beneath the cross. Both were to embody the new community, made up of men and women. The reality of the church, and that means a church led by men, changed the original tradition.

It is also already evident that serving and the diaconate very quickly became functions specifically associated with women and that the male members of the community were able to dissociate themselves from them. Serving and preaching, service and leadership in the community were torn apart.

However, behind the masculine facade of the Gospel of Mark, the losers are still the victors. We can still see flashes there of the earlier preferential status of women.

Women, religion and women's rights

Women and religion are particularly closely related. This conviction unites misogynists and those favourable to women. Women fill the churches. According to a common view, expressed here by Peter Ketter, women have 'a natural gift of sensitivity', by virtue of which they 'recognized the divine in Jesus of Nazareth more quickly than men'. Women are regarded as being more capable of enthusiasm, more spontaneous, more emotional; they have more sensitive antennae and seem to be primarily receptive to the numinous and the religious.

The group of women in the New Testament has always been a reflection of a person's own view of women. By contrast, the apostles take on something of a timeless quality. To compare them with a dining club, a lodge, a men's association, would be regarded as blasphemy, and is a view to be found only among critics of religion. The group of women is not seen like this: they are regarded as the 'group of women from Galilee', as servants, as a diaconate, as the first Christian women's movement. This understanding of them, which changes with the times, extends even to translations of the Bible: whereas earlier they were 'serving' women, now they are 'caring' women. The diaconal element is detached from bourgeois ideals. However, these adapted translations also lose the New Testament connection between Jesus and the women. The 'service' for which Jesus came and which the women continue cannot be described in terms of caring hospitality.

Luke had day-dreams of women with great resources. Ernest Renan idealized them, in accordance with the world of the nineteenth-century salon, as sensitive conversation partners who enthusiastically attached themselves to Jesus: 'He (Jesus) conveyed to them that pre-eminent restraint which makes possible a very attractive community of ideas between both sexes. They introduced into the new sect an element of enthusiasm and of the miraculous, the importance of which was already understood at the time.'

In the 1960s, the women in the rock opera *Jesus Christ Superstar* took on a psychological, therapeutic function with their comforting song 'Everything's Alright'. Today, they are sometimes detected as having a bent towards emancipation. Alongside concern for the group of men there is already independence: in Barreau's biography of Jesus, women open their mouths and say provocative things. In the revolutionary situation in Nicaragua, women rediscover a parallel situation to the time of Jesus: the same courage, the same pluck which sets women now, as then, above men and enables them to withstand revolution. There is some justification in these interpretations, which could be continued at will, especially if they come from those involved and help towards self-discovery and identification. Perhaps it would even have been a good thing also to keep reinterpreting the group of disciples and to use them to kindle changing social visions, instead of seeing them as images of church leaders, strong in faith, persistent, and always filled with the Holy Spirit. However, these should not be models intended to be followed, invented by others and slanted to produce the desired effect in the person affected.

For many people the situation becomes critical only when rights, social and theological consequences are inferred from the specific perspective of a feminist group. To reward the apparently emotional advantage of women with special privileges provokes opposition. As a counter-attack it is said that women's household duties are burden enough, without their being actively involved in, say, the church's official ministry, and that they have too little interest in the 'what and why and wherefore'. As Ketter says, 'So long as they love. There is no doubt at all about their ministry: to care for him, to serve him, to stand under his cross'.

The preferential role of *individual* women in the gospel has always been noted. Alongside the great unknown woman, whom many theologians allow to be wiser and more far-sighted than all the disciples, there are women who believe *for* others, like the Syro-Phoenician woman (Mark 7.24ff.) or the Samaritan woman (John 4.1ff.). Women become the first witnesses of the resurrection, although according to Jewish law the testimony of women was not valid.

Mary Magdalene becomes the apostle of all apostles, and despite all attacks, was able to maintain this role right down to the Middle Ages.

The conflict arises when people see women as a *group* with special rights, with a culture and story of their own in the gospel. As a male, Mereschkowski could still affirm with full authority: 'The weak women are stronger than the men: the faith of Peter the rock ran away like sand; the faith of Mary, however, was truly a rock. The love of men proved powerless; the love of women was strong. The sun of man's love sets in

death, but the sun of woman's love arises in the resurrection.'
A woman who noted the same thing wrote rather too enthusiastically about the Stations of the Cross: 'At the sixth and
eighth stations the triumphal course of the women begins. It
goes beyond the bloody climax of Calvary, where the faithfulness of women keeps watch over the dying and the dead, to the
light of Easter morning and through all the centuries down to
our own day. Where men retreated, fled and hid themselves in
fear and trembling, there stands the woman, called and led by
her compassionate heart, full of faithfulness and surrender.'
However, this provoked powerful masculine aggression. In an
article, 'Rescuing Male Honour at Golgotha', a correction was
made to the exegetical 'error' with a reference to the evangelist
Luke, who has both women *and* men present under the cross
and knows of no flight by the disciples. The 'touching love' of
women is assigned its proper place: 'The touching fidelity and
dependence of the pious women on the Master does not suffer
the least loss if we do not contrast it with the behaviour of the
disciples. It has become so customary to speak only of the faithful women under the cross, and of the cowardly men who fled,
that it is necessary to rescue male honour.'

In our patriarchal church and theology we probably have no
need to rescue men's honour. Where such an attempt is made in
a vociferous way, we tend, rather, to find feelings of guilt and
anxiety. The predominant view is that all are sinners, all are
the same and there are no 'ladies first' in the church.

Even the great teachers of religion, the painters of the pre-
Reformation period, who have shaped all of us, preferred to
harmonize rather than provoke. Thus they portray patrons,
bishops and protectors under the cross, or at least the beloved
disciple, told of by the later, stylized, Gospel of John. Obviously
there were also always women there. However, hardly any
artists painted the story of Jesus correctly from a historical
point of view, and they were rarely interested in rescuing female
honour. Thus the pictures suggest to us that there is no

differentiation between men and women. Here women's experiences have been forgotten. It is hard for values to be communicated where there are no rights.

Hardly anyone is aware that 'we' always think, theologize, paint and pray from the perspective of the disciples. A passion prayer, 'Lord Jesus, your people have rejected you, all your friends have forsaken you . . .' displays this impregnable masculine bastion about which people hardly ever reflect. The theological consequences are that the abyss between God and man always remains open, in a deliberate, paralysing way. A parallel feminine prayer would run: 'We tried to be with you but we could not help you. We feel our helplessness, but your nearness. We try to participate in the suffering of this world . . .'

Here community and responsibility could grow in a new way. The division about which masculine theology teaches us could be healed and filled out with other human experiences. The rediscovery of the unique role of women in history, theology and the church would enrich both men and women.

The peasant women who learnt self-confidence from the Bible teach us self-confidence in our experiences as women in the church.

Two mothers of disciples
with their children

*Mary Salome and Mary
Cleopas.
The Sigmaringen Master.*

6

MATTHEW AND THE MOTHERS

Then the wife of Zebedee came to Jesus with her two sons, bowed before him, and asked him a favour. 'What do you want?' Jesus asked her. She answered, 'Promise me that these two sons of mine will sit at your right and your left when you are King.' 'You don't know what you are asking for,' Jesus answered the sons. 'Can you drink the cup of suffering that I am about to drink?' 'We can,' they answered. 'You will indeed drink from my cup,' Jesus told them, 'but I do not have the right to choose who will sit at my right and my left. These places belong to those for whom my Father has prepared them . . . If one of you wants to be first, he must be your slave, like the Son of Man, who did not come to be served, but to serve and to give his life to redeem many people' (Matt. 20.20–23.27f.).

Then Jesus went with his disciples to a place called Gethsemane, and he said to them, 'Sit here while I go over there and pray.' He took with him Peter and the two sons of Zebedee . . . Then the armed men came up, arrested Jesus, and held him tight . . . Then all the disciples left him and ran away (Matt. 26.36f., 50, 56).

When the army officer and the soldiers with him who were watching Jesus saw the earthquake and everything else that happened, they were terrified and said, 'He really was the Son of God.' There were many women there, looking on from a distance, who had followed Jesus from Galilee and helped him. Among them were Mary Magdalene, Mary the mother of James and Joseph, and the wife of Zebedee (Matt. 27.54–56).

Salome's task was not an easy one. Her boys James and John were boisterous characters; Jesus later called them 'sons of thunder', because this boisterousness also revealed itself at a later date. Their mother did not succeed in eradicating this passion from their hearts. Jesus was the first to do this with the discipline of his spirit and the power of his love. To bring up such boisterous youths is no easy or light task for a mother. So often a mother's heart is weak, and she gives in to the children. Yet it is very important in the first years of a child that his will should be broken and that his stubborn head should be made to bow (Ernst Modersohn).

Thus Salome is a splendid model for the mother of any priest (Peter Ketter).

The old order falls apart

What does a man do when he sees that women have suddenly become independent? When he sees that women, who were originally in the background, deliberately come into the fore-ground? When the old order, that men should speak and women keep silent, falls apart?

Matthew – as we call the author of the first Gospel – experienced this feminine revolution in the early communities. He was a Jew, and presumably had conservative attitudes. Women did not have much to say in the synagogue worship which he knew. That was in accord with the times. Usually they sat silently in their segregated places, while men and male children could be called upon to read from the holy scriptures. 'A woman does not read from the Torah because of the honour of the community.' Of course, there are indications that even here women already had the right to join in the talking and the decision-making, in the same way as Hellenistic women. However, there is much evidence to suggest that in most communities the women were still trained to keep silence. They had to listen to the liturgy, the thanksgivings and the confessions of faith. They were allowed only to say simple prayers, like grace over meals at home. And according to the views of some rabbis, those who were kept quiet did not need any religious instruction. On the contrary, that could be dangerous. One teacher warned, 'Anyone who teaches his daughter the law, teaches her folly.'

Now in many new Christian communities Matthew sees precisely the opposite: women preach, go on missionary journeys and are called apostles. They direct communities and instruct women, children and even men in the new teaching. Thus Priscilla instructs Apollos, a fellow-worker with Paul, who is later to be an apostle. An opponent of Christianity even goes so far as to assert that the church is ruled by women and that women assign ministries in the church.

In many respects women are quicker and more imaginative than men. This will later be held against them, and will be regarded as ecstatic language. Furthermore, they have the great advantage that some of their number had close contact with Jesus, had seen him as the risen Lord and had been commissioned to proclaim him. These women were convinced that they were authentic witnesses to Jesus, and many men found it difficult to cope with the fact that they had a secondary role in these communities. Thus a late gospel tells of a rivalry between Peter and Mary Magdalene. To some degree there was a real partnership: men and women shared all the tasks between them. However, masculine aggression also grew alongside this: according to the old biblical creation stories, did not men come first? Were they not the strong ones? Were they not the rulers?

The new customs were not questioned in communities made up of converted Greeks. The Greek women brought ideas of freedom into the communities. They no longer wore veils, like most Jewish women. They were independent, could be engaged in business, were familiar with festivals for women and feminine religious cults. In the new Christian communities they rediscovered the independence which they had already experienced in their own world. And in many stories in the Christian tradition women were regarded as the real disciples. This new religion met the needs of the new woman.

Matthew the Jew had to cope with this feminine phenomenon. He had before him the traditional story of Jesus, which was first written down by Mark. This was intended above all for those who were not Jews. He wanted to tell the story of Jesus all over again, in his own way, and in terms of his own understanding of Jesus, to the Jewish communities among whom he lived. And he wanted to win over Jews to the cause of Jesus. For him, Jesus was the new king of Israel who rejected his own people in favour of the new people, the new church, a community made up of Jews and Gentiles. Matthew wanted to use this notion to bind together old and new stories of Jesus.

Such a book represented a profound departure from the centuries-old traditions of Judaism. Matthew accepted this challenge. However, where it did not seem to him to be absolutely necessary, he made compromises. He simply retained traditional Jewish laws which Jesus had deliberately broken: for example, the laws relating to purity.

Because of his character and his upbringing, he found the stories about the women in the Gospel of Mark, which are also told elsewhere, hard to take. But they were so much a part of the gospel, of the message of the new church which was his concern, that he could not ignore them. In his Gospel, too, the disciples flee. In his Gospel, too, the women stand beneath the cross, are at the tomb, and witness the resurrection. Matthew could not avoid this tradition, and did not want to. However, he introduced a few coloured threads of his own into the picture with which he was confronted.

122

A Jewish mother finds liberation

When a man comes across a new type of woman who confuses him and makes him unsure, he measures her in some way by his mother. He compares the two, and if he is open, he may find features of his mother in the new woman. If this is unsuccessful, he will lament his lost image of women and his lost mother, and be unable to find access to a new generation of women.

Matthew, too, has an image of his mother to heart. Presumably he had a concerned, competent, ambitious mother or wife. He looks at the Jewish wives and mothers around him and measures by them those women in Mark's story who are mothers, or at least maternal. And in this way he conjures up the picture of the loving Jewish mother who concentrates on her family, and incorporates this into his Gospel, to help himself and others.

The central story is the brief episode with the mother of the disciples. A woman falls on her knees before Jesus. With some embarrassment, she asks him whether she may make a request. Her two grown sons stand beside her, irritated and at least as embarrassed as she is. The whole thing looks like a plot, which is ill-contrived and doomed to failure from the start. Jesus encourages the woman to make her request, and she asks for what all mothers of all times have desired for their children, respect and success: 'Promise me that my two sons will sit on your right and your left when you come into your kingdom.'

Had the sons put their mother up to this? Were all three vexed at Peter, who always seemed to be the favourite? Had the mother thought that she could get something out of Jesus more easily than her sons? According to Matthew, the three must somehow have plotted together and have had a close relationship. The amazing thing now is that Jesus does not honour this motherly concern in any way; he takes no notice of the mother, rightly snubs her and turns to her sons. 'You do

123

not know what you are asking.' Then he clearly tells them that to share with him and his cause involves suffering, and that unlike a feudal lord he cannot grant a share in his rule.

Who is this woman whom Matthew inserts here into a story which has already been told by Mark? In Mark, the disciples present the request by themselves. Matthew calls her the mother of the sons of Zebedee. These are James and John, members of the innermost group of disciples, characterized by a somewhat unruly temperament. Jesus called them the 'sons of thunder'. Zebedee himself was in charge of a large fishing business on Lake Gennesaret, which employed workers as well as his own sons.

The two disciples later became well-known leaders of communities in the early church. James became the first martyr among the apostles under Agrippa I (Acts 12.2); John is often named alongside Peter in the New Testament and presumably died a natural death. Like her sons, the wife of Zebedee was probably involved with the group of men and women from the beginnings of the Jesus movement, and remained with Jesus at least until the crucifixion (Matt. 27.56).

The wife of Zebedee entered the tradition as Salome. Matthew and Mark tell of three women under the cross: Matthew calls one of them 'the mother of the sons of Zebedee'. Mark calls one 'Salome'. It has been inferred from this that the two women were identical, and so the mother of the disciples has been called Salome. Another conjecture is that she was a sister of the mother of Jesus, because John has a sister of Mary standing beneath the cross (19.25). In the Middle Ages, the two were combined so as to be members of a holy clan and family, to which other biblical figures also belonged. A carved altar from the late Middle Ages shows all the mothers in this clan with their children and kinsfolk in a great family portrait: in the centre is Mary with the boy Jesus. On her right and her left are two mothers of disciples, each with two babies, later to become disciples, on their arms.

124

If we rule out these combinations and conjectures, we are left with two terse but informative pieces of information about the wife of Zebedee. In the Gospel of Matthew she intercedes for her sons, and she stands beneath the cross. What did the evangelist mean to convey by this?

Matthew makes a woman leave her family, her husband and her occupation to follow Jesus, the wandering preacher. Thus the group of Galilean women which we already know presents us with a new face. A mother, with all the typical characteristics of a mother, begins to follow Jesus. We know the mother of just one other disciple, Mary Cleopas, who stands beneath the cross, but that is all we know of her. Otherwise the private family relationships of the women who follow Jesus are completely unknown.

If Mark makes a sharp contrast between the disciples who fail to understand and the women who do, Matthew makes this woman share in the mistakes of the disciples. He smoothes down the sharp edges. However, that is perhaps not his real purpose. Perhaps he prefers to depict a woman in all her femininity and naturalness, the woman who lives her life in the persons of her children and merely wants the best for them.

Jewish women enjoyed great respect as mothers and above all as mothers of sons: 'Her sons rise up and call her blessed,' we read in the book of Proverbs. 'Truly, sons are the gift of Yahweh, the reward of the fruit of the womb; like arrows in the hand of the hero are young sons. Blessed is the man whose quiver is full of them,' enthuses the Psalmist. In addition to the widespread longing for a male to carry on the heritage, there was also the messianic hope for the birth of the Messiah. This hope permeates the whole of the Old Testament, makes childless women sink into deep despair and fills pregnant women with hopes that go far beyond their own persons. Perhaps in this respect the social and religious value of a Jewish mother who had borne sons was very different from that to be found in surrounding cultures

A mother who sees her whole worth embodied in her sons would also want to see public recognition given to them. The woman is nothing in her own right. She exists in her sons. Perhaps she is not concerned at all for riches and power. She speaks of the kingdom that she hopes for. She has heard the proclamation of the kingdom, of the rule of the Messiah and the new order in which the poor, the sinners and the Gentiles have pride of place. In Mark the disciples dream of 'glory'. *They* would like spiritual honours, and these would probably reflect on her.

She is a mother and lives in her children. Her request is apparently unselfish, yet it is for something quite foolish. She is really unconcerned for herself, yet her view is in a quite false perspective. She has left everyone in the lurch – perhaps even her husband – and yet she still clings on to that to which society attaches value for her, her sons.

Jesus simply ignores her. He does not take her at all seriously. Generously, he passes over her narrow-mindedness. He does not want this officious, vicarious motherliness. He wants her as a person. So he immediately turns to her sons and talks to them. Jesus does not encourage any mother cult, even towards his own mother. The first two Gospels at least are agreed over this. 'He who does the will of my Father who is in heaven is my brother, my sister and my mother' (Matt. 12.50).

It is only Luke, telling the Christmas story, who begins with veneration of Mary, which was still unknown in the first period of the church.

Matthew does not end the story of the wife of Zebedee with a disappointing rebuff. He places her beneath the cross with the familiar group of women. The mother of the sons of Zebedee, who fled so shamefully – like all the others – (Matt. 26.56), has now become herself. She has not espoused the cause of her sons. She has done more than leave her husband to follow Jesus. She is now without a family, from which she derived her sense of being valued. She has exchanged the places of spiritual

126

honour, which seemed to her so desirable, for the place of execution. She has acted differently from her sons and exposed herself to the danger of arrest. A woman has gone her own way. The group of women is now her only support. She is among those who truly follow Jesus. She has done what Jesus told her sons. A mother has emancipated herself. Perhaps deliberately, Matthew does not mention her name. Is she simply meant to be the example of a mother?

She has not made much of a mark on history and the history of art. In mediaeval art she appears as the cheerful mother of twins. In modern times she has been seen as the restrictive Protestant mother or the 'mother of the priest', depending on the confessional context. Contemporary ideals of motherhood became the model. However, Mary the mother of Jesus and Mariology soon forced her into the background and did not allow her to become even a maternal saint.

The ghetto is opened up

Matthew still does not see Mary as the ideal mother. He scatters motherhood and the typical conduct of a mother, from love to intransigence, throughout his Gospel: he depicts maternal influence behind the scenes in the person of the wife of Herod, who incites her daughter to ask for the head of John the Baptist by means of a seductive dance (14.8); he makes the Canaanite woman, who wants her mentally ill daughter to be healed, into an importunate hysterical mother, who pursues the group around Jesus with loud cries. In contrast to the story in Mark, Jesus first sends her away harshly and coldly: he has not come for the Gentiles, but for his own people, and in this way he mobilizes her entire energy and intelligence. Deeply impressed by this motherly tenacity, Jesus acknowledges her 'great faith' (15.28). He has two courageous mothers of disciples standing under the cross. But Mary, the mother of Jesus, is no more than an anxious young girl who has become pregnant,

127

and whose anxieties and concerns Matthew takes much less seriously than those of Joseph. This man, put in a shameful position, commands all his human sympathy. The birth narratives are stories about Joseph. Angels appear to Joseph, comfort him and explain to him his wife's incomprehensible pregnancy. In Luke, Mary stands in the foreground. In Matthew, the birth narrative still stands out from the patriarchal background, where the man makes history.

For Matthew, the world always remained a man's world. He takes a different view of the new ideas about marriage which Mark reports of Jesus (Mark 10.1ff.): he began from the view that only the *husband* could allow a divorce. He made a concession to men that they could divorce their wives in cases of immorality – and here that means adultery (5.32; 19.9). It went beyond his powers of imagining that a husband even had to forgive his unfaithful wife!

Matthew has opened up the ghetto of the woman still imprisoned in utterly conservative attitudes, just a little. He has shown that mothers may be themselves. He is also the only one to tell the story of Pilate's wife, who makes herself independent of her environment and gives her husband the sage advice not to have anything to do with the Jesus case. He describes the laborious process by which Jewish and also Gentile women free themselves. He introduced into Jesus' genealogy (Matt. 1) women who do not embody the honourable Jewish tradition, as do Sarah, Rebecca or Rachel. He replaces the mothers of the rich Jewish tradition with four women surrounded by scandal. Tamar secures her rights forcibly, becoming pregnant by her father-in-law. Rahab is a prostitute, conceals Israelite spies and helps the Israelite army to victory. Bathsheba is the beautiful wife of Uriah whom David sends out to battle on a fatal foray so that he can marry her; and Ruth is a loyal daughter-in-law, but at the same time a refined woman who uses skill to win her second husband.

All were thought to be beautiful, wise, competent and

deceitful; they were Gentiles or had Gentile connections, and gave the serious genealogy of Jesus a somewhat adventurous aspect. At the same time, the story of their personal scandals was always connected with a turning point in the salvation history of Israel: conquest, purchase of land, monarchy.

Did Matthew mean in this way to divert the stain which at this time still attached to Mary, on to the primal mothers? The maternal ancestors of his Messiah are a break with convention and the traditional image of women, and open up to the Gentile, the prostitute and those who are discriminated against the possibility of seeing themselves afresh and accepting the shadow of their history as salvation history.

In his portraits of mothers, Matthew continued to think, even when he came across the new self-confident women of the Hellenistic communities. But his mothers have judgments of their own; they run the risk of taking new steps, and have a personal history. Matthew attempted to understand the process of feminine emancipation laboriously, anxiously, in a masculine way, and was always ready to compromise. He tried to incorporate the new community made up of Jews and Gentiles, women and men, into his view of the world.

Here we can already see the difficulties which the Jewish Christian communities presented to the new woman's movement: a casuistic view of the law, a return to a patriarchal approach, concessions to misogynist traditions, even when they only concerned external matters like wearing veils. Like Paul, Matthew accepted the new social role of the woman, but did not advance it. In the long run the boundary post which both of them set up had a more powerful influence than the liberation with which they were already in agreement.

Joanna, Wife of Chuza.
Engraving by Adrian Collaert.

7

JOANNA, A LUCAN LADY

In many different ways John preached the Good News to the people and urged them to change their ways. But John reprimanded Herod, the governor, because he had married Herodias, his brother's wife, and had done many other evil things. Then Herod did an even worse thing by putting John into prison (Luke 3.18–20).

Some time later Jesus travelled through towns and villages, preaching the Good News about the Kingdom of God. The twelve disciples went with him, and so did some women who had been healed of evil spirits and diseases: Mary (who was called Magdalene), from whom seven demons had been driven out; Joanna, whose husband Chuza was an officer in Herod's court; and Suzanna, and many other women who used their own resources to help Jesus and his disciples (Luke 8.1–3).

When Herod, the ruler of Galilee, heard about all the things that were happening, he was very confused, because some people were saying that John the Baptist had come back to life . . . Herod said, 'I had John's head cut off; but who is this man I hear these things about?' And he kept trying to see Jesus (Luke 9.7f.).

At the same time some Pharisees came to Jesus and said to him,

131

'You must get out of here and go somewhere else, because Herod wants to kill you' (Luke 13.31).

When Pilate learnt that Jesus was from the region ruled by Herod, he sent him to Herod, who was also in Jerusalem at that time. Herod was very pleased when he saw Jesus, because he had heard about him and had been wanting to see him for a long time. He was hoping to see Jesus perform some miracle. So Herod asked Jesus many questions, but Jesus made no answer. The chief priests and the teachers of the Law stepped forward and made strong accusations against Jesus. Herod and his soldiers mocked Jesus and treated him with contempt; then they put a fine robe on him and sent him back to Pilate. On that very day Herod and Pilate became friends; before this they had been enemies (Luke 23.7–12).

Very early on Sunday morning the women went to the tomb, carrying the spices they had prepared. They found the stone rolled away from the entrance to the tomb, so they went in; but they did not find the body of the lord Jesus. They stood there puzzled about this, when suddenly two men in bright shining clothes stood by them. Full of fear, the women bowed down to the ground, as the men said to them, 'Why are you looking among the dead for one who is alive? He is not here, he has been raised. Remember what he said to you while he was in Galilee: "The Son of Man must be handed over to sinful men, be crucified, and three days later rise to life." ' Then the women remembered his words, returned from the tomb, and told all these things to the eleven disciples and all the rest. The women were Mary Magdalene, Joanna, and Mary the mother of James; they and the other women with them told these things to the apostles. But the apostles thought that what the women said was nonsense, and they did not believe them (Luke 24.1 11).

132

JOANNA, A LUCAN LADY

We do not know a woman disciple called Joanna from Holy Scripture (Werner Ross in the *Frankfurter Allgemeine Zeitung*, 1978).

Joanna left her home and followed him, so that she could always be close to him. Either she did this with the consent of her husband, or Chuza was already dead when Jesus Christ entered her home (Gerhard Eis).

One day she saw Jesus. She listened to him, left her husband, her home and her slaves, and went with Jesus through the countryside, the villages and the ports in the motley throng which attached itself to him. She spent the night with the foxes and the ravens. For the first time she was not someone's wife, but a woman: Joanna, an authentic person (Jörg Zink).

Joanna, an authentic person

Hardly anyone knows Joanna. Theologians in their studies never meet her, and they have ignored her in biblical texts. A journalist discussing a modern biography of Jesus mocked the 'fabrication' of a woman disciple called Joanna. She often does not appear at all in books about women of the Bible, and when she does, she is quickly passed over.

What is the reason for this? Are the two notes about her in Luke too brief? But Joseph of Arimathea, those who play dice beneath the cross, the disciple who fled naked at Jesus' arrest, are mentioned equally briefly, and yet they have stimulated the imagination and have also found a place in literature.

Was Joanna a woman whose story was not very productive? But the mother of the sons of Zebedee, likewise, is mentioned only twice and yet is generally known.

The material here is explosive. A woman from court society, the wife of a senior royal official, following Jesus! What a sensation! The social middle-class of the Jesus group,

133

consisting of craftsmen and dependents, takes on splendour and respect. A theme for the popular papers and the gossips of all times! A woman who gives up a rich, secure life at the side of an influential man and shares in the risky and penurious life of a popular figure and social revolutionary. What material for romances!

But this is presumably the reason why people forgot Joanna: her story was a painful one. She is introduced as the wife of a distinguished man whom she left. Of course on Reformation Sunday, the church sings,

> Although they take our life,
> goods, honour, children, wife

but it does not allow that one could possibly give up goods, honour, children and *husband* for the sake of Jesus. Joanna is a scandalous figure in the New Testament. Women who sinned and committed adultery could at least expect some understanding. But a woman who left her husband was a scandal that was better swept under the table. The best justification for this assumption seems to me to be the zeal of our theologians, concerned for the integrity of the family, to assume that Chuza, the finance minister, was dead. In that case there would be an honourable widow who put her superfluous strength at the service of the church and corresponded to the model Christian woman of all ages. Or it was presupposed that her husband agreed that Joanna should follow Jesus – a somewhat shallow view, since a little later the person who invented it again speaks of the 'widow'.

Of course the mother of the sons of Zebedee aroused maternal feelings. Joanna's story was dangerous, and there was a preference to keep women at arms' length. The rare occasions on which she was painted found her represented with the flask of oil (this vessel being the symbol of the woman), now turned into a feminine symbol, and loving gifts. To this day in the Catholic church she has been the patron saint of those providing for convents. However, the inflammatory elements in her story were avoided. She was reduced to the loving, caring woman, whom people needed.

Who was Joanna? What is her story? Where does she come into contact with the story of women today?

We do not know much about her. Was she beautiful, rich, tired of the harem when she decided to follow Jesus? Or was she sick, no longer attractive enough for court ceremonies, or to be a representative of her husband?

The court of king Herod, to which she belonged, does not have a good reputation in biblical narratives. The Herod concerned is the son of Herod the Great, well known as the man who ordered the killing of the children of Bethlehem. His father was a foreigner, of Idumaean descent; he was successful and brought stability to the kingdom of Judaea, though he was not very popular among the Jews because he was a usurper. His son Herod Antipas inherited part of the kingdom; he was in control of the territory within which Jesus was active, and proved much less significant than his father: he was later dethroned and exiled. He built a residence for himself at Tiberias, on Lake Gennesaret, and it is there that Joanna will have had her scintillating experience of court life. Whereas Herod the Great had a harem of ten wives, Joanna's lord was marked out by his passion for one woman. Her name was Herodias, and she was his niece and sister-in-law, whom he estranged from his half-brother and for whom he put away his first wife. John the Baptist evidently condemned this very strongly. Matthew and Mark have portrayed the dramatic scene in which Herodias' daughter Salome, whom Herodias had kept with her in her new marriage, danced before her stepfather and the court with such seduction that Herod, deeply affected, promised that he would fulfil her wish. Salome asked for the head of John the Baptist. Herodias, wounded by the Baptist and publicly shamed, had taken her revenge in suggesting the request to her daughter. Was Joanna also a spectator at this dance? Did she watch while the bloody dish with the head of the great preacher of repentance was presented to the court?

The court was at least aware of the movements focussing on John and Jesus. Herod was not really ill-disposed towards them. He was personally wounded by the moral preaching of the Baptist and had him killed because his wife forced him to. But he was more curious about the Jesus movement than hostile towards it. He had heard stories of miracles and wanted to see them for himself. He was even 'delighted' to see Jesus, though he was then disappointed that Jesus did not show him anything. Presumably one of the miracles he had heard about was the healing of the minister's wife.

Chuza and Joanna lived in this atmosphere of lust, caprice, wealth and whim, indifference and open curiosity. Joanna's encounter with Jesus and her healing introduced her for the first time to something else: an independent life without whim, with a purpose; a community of men and women from different levels of society who dealt with one another in complete freedom and from whom healing powers emanated. Joanna left her husband to begin a new life of her own. She was no pitiful ascetic, who left everything behind her. She brought wealth of her own, and in the Jesus group remained what she was, a respectable woman with influence and capital. The only difference was that she had won her freedom. Perhaps she brought some prosperity and comfort to the group around Jesus; she has been credited with providing Jesus with the valuable garment that he wore, woven in one piece, and that the soldiers later shared among themselves. The unguents to be used for the embalming are a luxury which would not come within the usual experience of fishermen's wives. Good meals and comfortable room for the Last Supper have also been attributed to Joanna's initiative. The penurious Jesus movement took on some elegance. Joanna remains herself, but is free from old ties, from the experience of arbitrariness and servitude between husband and wife.

136

JOANNA, A LUCAN LADY

In his book *Les mémoires de Jesus*, the French priest Jean Claude Barreau makes Joanna the leading light among the group of women and is one of the first to rediscover her as a person. Whereas he leaves the 'faithful' Martha and 'sinful' Mary Magdalene in their traditional roles, he makes Joanna the representative of emancipation. Jesus had promised his wife Sarah, who had died early, on her deathbed that he would fight against the foolish prejudices of society which always regarded women as inferior to men. It was only out of respect for the mentality of the society of his time that Jesus had refrained from including a woman in his small group.

'She is a woman who knows what she wants,' Barreau makes Jesus say of Joanna, 'and she does not let anyone push her around. My disciples still cannot bear women treating them as equals, so it is not surprising that there were often vigorous quarrels.'

For Barreau, Joanna is a well-to-do, independent lady with good connections and her own views. She gives Judas, the treasurer, a certain sum of money each month. She is not afraid to join in discussions with the Pharisees, and tells the lawyers that it is wrong to allow husbands to divorce their wives for no good reasons. She is the leader of the group of women, as Peter is the leader of the group of men.

Here an attempt is made to give a new interpretation of a woman in the Bible. However, Barreau is still bound by traditional views of women; he gives the mother of Jesus too positive and too Catholic a role, which is not faithful enough to the Bible; he seems to make the women disappear before the arrest of Jesus; and he does not draw on the New Testament sufficiently in his tradition about the women around Jesus.

Jörg Zink, who uses the note about Joanna as the basis for a meditation on the freedom of a woman compared with that of her husband, makes no comment on the second mention of Joanna. In his view, no one has ever pronounced on the issue that it was reprehensible that from then on Peter ceased to

137

provide any income for his family. It was Jesus' will that women should do the same thing, and that means giving up all the housework! However, the political emphasis which Luke attaches to the story of Joanna makes her more than a weary housewife.

What significance does Joanna have for Luke, and what role does she play among the other women?

Joanna and Herod

Luke is fond of distinguished ladies, and it makes him proud to depict their social and financial background. But there is also something else about Joanna: she has a political background, which is not the case with any other of the women who followed Jesus. Four times, Luke brings this background into his story of Jesus. Four times the court of the local ruler is shown to be in conflict with the Jesus movement: the adultery of the ruler, his delight in sensations, his threat to murder Jesus, and finally the cynical scene in which the prisoner Jesus is made the object of the court's mockery. The curiosity and the involved interest of the family of Herod in the Jesus affair recurs in Acts: three grandchildren of Herod show the same kind of attitude as their grandfather. In Caesarea, Drusilla the granddaughter of Herod comes with her husband, the governor Felix, to Paul's prison to hear more about Jesus and the Christian faith. However, the two soon find Paul's serious preaching distasteful. Felix dismisses him with the words, 'You may leave now. I will call you again when I get the chance.' Conversations of this kind could therefore still have taken place (Acts 24).

Agrippa, the grandson of Herod, together with his sister Berenice, makes Paul give a public defence of himself before the whole court in the ceremonial audience chamber. Paul's passionate speech makes Agrippa reflect, 'Do you think that you can make a Christian of me so quickly?' Both times there are hesitations, doubts, sympathy from Herod's descendants In

JOANNA, A LUCAN LADY

the end, however, there is no decision in favour of the Jesus movement. Events are left to run their course, and that is in fact a negative verdict (Acts 24).

This special interest of Luke's in the family of Herod and the note that Joanna came from court society must be seen together. The radical decision of Joanna to leave her husband and the court and to follow Jesus stands in contrast with the half sympathy which turns from laxity and indecision into the opposition which forces the execution of Jesus. And Joanna is not just the one who provides prosperity and care. For Luke she is a member of the group of women from Galilee present at the crucifixion, and he makes special mention of her name in the resurrection scene. Whereas Herod shows solidarity with the Roman governor and in a cynical way delivers Jesus to Pilate and thus to certain death, Joanna shows solidarity with Jesus and takes the risk of being identified as the wife of the minister and a former member of the court. In contrast to a half-sympathy which thus proves to be negative, she embodies a total sympathy which risks everything. In contrast to social interest in new things, she does something new. What began in Galilee, at that time in close proximity to the court in Tiberias, here comes to fulfilment. The two angels recall the sayings of Jesus before his resurrection, that he originally uttered in Galilee. The way of Herod led from Galilee to Jerusalem. The way of Joanna leads from Galilee to Jerusalem. Here are two parallel lines which do not meet.

What happened to Joanna later is an open question, left to our imagination. The early community does not hand her name down to us. However, that does not tell against her historical existence. Presumably she could never free herself from her past. She remained in danger. No man seems to have taken the risk that she took in Jerusalem, a member of the court identifying herself with a traitor to the state. Nicodemus came by night. Joanna stands under the cross in the clear light of day, and comes to the tomb on Easter morning.

The emancipation of women in the male church

Luke inserts into the group of women an interesting figure who is not mentioned again in any other Gospel. He puts her on the same footing as the famous Mary Magdalene, and mentions the two with equal frequency. Elsewhere he has described women with a life-story and an individual personality of their own. He has given colour and individuality to the story of the women which in Mark is told briefly and impersonally, and in Matthew is still written from a patriarchal perspective. Mary, who in Matthew stayed in the background in favour of Joseph, disturbed and arousing our sympathy, now becomes the heroine of the birth narratives. Alongside her we find Zacharias, whose lips are sealed, and another pregnant woman, Elizabeth, the mother of John the Baptist. Luke speaks of prophetesses like Hanna and the daughters of Philip, and women entrepreneurs like Lydia, the dealer in purple dye; slaves who have gained their freedom, like Rhoda, and Tabitha, an imaginative seamstress in the service of the diaconate. His women are not stifled in partnership, but are mentioned alongside the husbands and – if they are more significant than the latter – are even mentioned before them, like Priscilla, the teacher of Paul's fellow-worker Apollos. They hear sermons by themselves, and are converted to Christianity without asking the permission of their husbands first. Of course they can also be equally fanatical opponents of the new religion. Luke brings women out of the shadows and assesses them as individuals.

At the same time, however, he has qualified the early practice of putting men and women on an equal footing. He either did not recognize the equality of ministries which is known to us from other communities, or was unaware of it. He transfers the Samaritan mission (Acts 8.5) to a man. According to the narrative in John (John 4), Jesus entrusted it to a woman. Martha, the friend of Jesus known from the first Christian community, had become too independent for him, perhaps too rich and self-centred, so he pushed her into the background. Like his predecessors, he still has the group of women under the cross. Now, however, there are other acquaintances there, so it is left open whether or not these were male followers of Jesus. The flight of the disciples is no longer given explicit mention.

The old stories about women which circulated in the earliest community have been changed. For Luke, the women are no longer the favoured disciples. It is a prostitute who now performs the anointing, the act of emancipation. We no longer have the wise woman anointing a king, a dead body, in contrast to the unknowing disciples. Furthermore, the women no longer serve Jesus – *he* serves them, because that is the reason why he has come into the world. They serve Jesus *and* the Twelve. It is the male disciples who stand apart, and who have a special relationship with Jesus. It is they who represent the tradition, and have a ministry and apostolic status.

In contrast to the group of women, this group of men is an elitist, celibate community. In Luke, renouncing one's possessions and leaving one's spouse are necessary preconditions for discipleship. In Mark and Matthew, the disciples are similarly required to break up the family and leave home. However, wives are an exception, and we keep hearing of spouses following Jesus (compare Luke 14.26 with Matt. 10.37ff.). In Matthew and Mark the people leave their old existence, but in Luke it is also said that they 'leave all' (Luke 5.11, 28).

The sayings of Jesus handed down by Luke, 'Sell your goods and give the money to the poor . . . No one can be my disciple unless he gives up everything . . .', do not fit in well with women like Mary Magdalene, Joanna and Susanna, who have possessions. They relate merely to the historical disciples of Jesus. But for Luke, no women belonged to this group. An ascetic, monastic, masculine ideal slipped into the church. The women were not female disciples.

Now Luke is a doctor and practitioner and knows that this is not the ideal by which a church is built up. He is writing

about AD 60. He is the second generation. The communities
have adapted to the social structures of the surrounding world.
The ideal of the historical disciples is a norm for which the
communities should strive, but it does not represent the rule.
By contrast, what Luke describes through the group of women
around Jesus is the practical ideal for the community: to keep
half one's possessions, be generous, and take the part of the
weak. The social aim is a sharing out of possessions within
the community, and Luke illustrated this by the group of
women and their service towards Jesus and the penniless disciples. For him, the group of women are the flesh-and-blood
embodiment of discipleship. For all his flirting with the poor,
Luke is a preacher to the rich and gives them ethical instruc-
tions on how they should use their money. He looked for
concrete solutions, and one firm fact for him was probably that
women have different tasks from men.

Luke envisages a church with many practical tasks: social
concerns which were alien in the world in which he lived, looking after widows and the poor. Work had to be found for
widows, and community service had to be organized. This was
closest to his heart, and it was for these services that he emancipated the women in the church: diaconia, the leading of
house churches, and prophecy. It was apostles and presbyters
who handed on the tradition. A woman had no prospects here.
But in the new community she was offered an abundance of
new tasks which would be almost beyond her resources. It was
here that she could develop, and here he saw her tasks for his
time.

Luke, who is always portrayed as being so well-disposed
towards women, proves disappointing. His church is the
church of the next two thousand years: ruled by men and
served by women. In his time, ministries of women are still a
revolution. But in a church which does not always see the
question of women anew as a challenge, they prove to be
stagnation. However, the revolutionary potential which Luke

142

discovered in women could also do away again with all church structures which have compromised with the times.

Luke himself reported one of the finest healings of a woman, which in this way points beyond itself (13.10ff.). It is the sabbath. All activity is prohibited. Jesus is in the synagogue and his glance falls on a woman who is doubled up with paralysis. She cannot even look up. He calls her to him and heals her, and she can stand up straight again. When the rulers of the synagogue protest that it is the sabbath and that such action is forbidden, Jesus replies that this woman too is a daughter of Abraham.

This small episode is more profound than it seems. The crippled woman is not just an old churchgoer, tormented by gout or arthritis, which is the way in which she is usually portrayed. The fact that she cannot look up also means for Luke that she has no hope, cannot raise her head and see the approach of redemption. He uses the same word, *anakuptein*, look up, as he does in the sentence, 'Look up and lift up your heads, because your redemption is approaching' (Luke 21.28). The remark about 'standing upright again' also has a double sense. It has a parallel in the saying about weary knees and tired hands, which are to be lifted up with the hope of Christ (Isa. 35.3; Heb. 12.12). Crippling of the body is at the same time a crippling of the soul.

For the first time we now have the saying about the daughter of Abraham, which goes beyond all previous hopes of salvation oriented on men. If up to that point the expectations of salvation were bound up in the male progeny, the son, on whose shoulders rule was to rest (Isa. 9.5), now the daughter has taken her place alongside the son with equal rights, and equal rights to inheritance. Between two healings of men on the sabbath (6.6ff.; 14.1ff.), Luke tells of the healing of a woman on the sabbath. In Jesus the woman has gained salvation and hope, an upright walk and a future. She can look up; she can see the coming order. This story already breaks the

bounds of the anxious, pragmatic ecclesiastical solutions which
Luke provides elsewhere, and points beyond them to a church
of men and women who can stand upright, enjoying equal
status.

Two women

Mary Magdalene and Martha.
Jacob Acker, Ulm. Fifteenth century.

BIBLIOGRAPHY

Barreau, Jean Claude, *Les mémoires de Jesus*, Paris 1978
Ben Chorim, Shalom, *Bruder Jesus*, Munich 1977
Brown, Raymond E., 'Roles of Women in the Fourth Gospel',
    Theological Studies 36, 4, Baltimore 1975
Bücher, Karl, *Die Frauenfrage im Mittelalter*, Tübingen 1970
Bultmann, Rudolf, *The Gospel of John*, Blackwell and West-
    minster Press, Philadelphia 1971
Cardenal, Ernesto, *The Gospel in Solentiname*, Orbis Books,
    Maryknoll, New York 1976–9
Eckhart, Meister, *Ewige Geburt*, Gütersloh 1948
Eggimann, Ernst, *Jesustexte*, Zurich 1972
Eis, Gerhard, 'Johanna', in *Unsere Namenspatrone im Wort und
    Bild*, Munich nd.
Grundmann, Herbert, *Religiöse Bewegungen im Mittelalter*,
    Darmstadt 1970
Hansel, Hans, *Die Maria Magdalena-Legende*, Bottrop 1937
Janssen, Marga, *Maria Magdalena in der abendländischen
    Kunst*, Freiburg Dissertation 1961
Jelsma, Auke, *Heilige und Hexen*, Constance 1977
Jewett, Paul K., *Man as Male and Female*, Eerdmans, Grand
    Rapids 1975
Ketter, Peter, *Christ and Womankind*, Newman Press, Mary-
    land 1952
Koch, Gottfried, *Frauenfrage und Ketzertum im Mittelalter*,
    Berlin 1962
Künstle, Karl, *Ikonografie der christlicher Kunst*, Freiburg 1926
Leipoldt, Johannes, *Die Frau in der antiken Welt und im
    Urchristentum*, Leipzig 1955

BIBLIOGRAPHY

Luther, Martin, *Werke*, Weimarer Ausgabe 28, 449, 32, 35
Luthi, Karl, and Hartmann, Walther, 'Theologie der Zärtlich-
keit', *Radius* 2, May 1979
Maillet, Germaine, *L'Art et les Saints: Saint Marthe*, Paris 1932
Mereschkowski, D. S., *Tod und Auferstehung*, Leipzig 1935
Modersohn, Ernst, *Die Frauen des Neuen Testaments*, Berlin
1958
Moltmann, Elisabeth (ed.), *Frauenbefreiung – Biblische und
theologische Argumente*, Munich 1978
—, 'Die Frauen im Neuen Testament', *Freiheit, Gleichheit,
Schwesterlichkeit*, Munich 1976
Neumann, E., 'Die Bedeutung des Erdarchetyps fur die Neu-
zeit', *Eranosjahrbuch* 1953
—, *The Great Mother. An Analysis of the Archetype*, Princeton
University Press 1972
Parvey, Constance F., 'The Theology and Leadership of
Women in the New Testament', in *Religion and Sexism.
Images of Women in the Jewish and Christian Traditions*, ed.
Rosemary Radford Ruether, Harper and Row, New York
1974
Phipps, William, *Was Jesus Married?*, Harper and Row 1970
Rengstorf, K. H., *Das Evangelium nach Lukas*, Göttingen 1937
Rice, Tim, with Webber, Andrew Lloyd, *Jesus Christ Superstar*,
Leeds Music 1970
Rudiger, Gertrud von, 'Magdaleneliteratur vom Mittelalter bis
zur Gegenwart', *Die Frau*, Berlin, 18th year 1911, pp. 464ff.
Russell, Letty, *The Liberating Word*, Westminster Press,
Philadelphia 1976
Schelkle, K. H., *Der Geist und die Braut*, Düsseldorf 1977
Schiller, Gertrud, *Ikonographie der christlichen Kunst* (four
vols.), Gütersloh 1971f.
Schniewind, Julius, *Das Evangelium nach Markus*, Göttingen
1949
Schottroff, Luise, and Stegemann, Wolfgang, *Jesu von Nazareth,
Hoffnung der Armen*, Stuttgart 1978

Schüssler-Fiorenza, Elisabeth, 'The Twelve', in *Women Priests*, ed. L. and A. Swidler, Paulist Press, New York 1977

Schweizer, Eduard, *The Good News according to Mark*, SPCK and John Knox Press, Atlanta 1970

—, *Jesus*, SCM Press and John Knox Press, Atlanta 1971

Stagg, Evelyn and Frank, *Women in the World of Jesus*, Westminster Press, Philadelphia 1978

Strunk, Reiner, *Menschen am Kreuzweg*, Stuttgart 1977

Swidler, L., 'Jesus was a Feminist', *Catholic World*, January 1971, 177–83

Thrade, Klaus, 'Arger mit der Freiheit', in *Freunde in Christus werden*, ed. G. Schaffenorth, Gelnhausen 1977

Thyen, Hartwig, 'nicht mehr mannlich noch weiblich', in *Als Mann und Frau geschaffen*, ed. G. Schaffenorth, Gelnhausen 1978

Voragine, Jacobus de, *Die legenda aurea*, Heidelberg 1979

Wolff, Hanna, *Jesus der Mensch*, Radius Verlag 1977

Zink, Jorg, *Sag mir wohin*, Stuttgart 1977

'Martha', 'Maria Magdalena', *Lexikon der Ikonografie*, Freiburg 1974